The

LATE GREAT
United States

Rachelle C. Hood

Freedom LINE BOOKS
SEE YOU AT THE FREEDOM LINE.

Book Three: The Late Great United States

CONTENTS

"Write the vision and make it plain on tablets that he may run who reads it. For the vision is yet for an appointed time; but at the end it will speak, and it will not lie. Though it tarries, wait for it; because it will surely come, it will not tarry."

(Habakkuk 2:2-3)

Prologue

"Behold, I am against you, O Tyre ….

He will direct his battering rams against your walls, and with axes he will break down your towers. Because of the abundance of his horses, their dust will cover you; your walls will shake at the noise of the horsemen, the wagons, and the chariots, when he enters your gates, as men enter a city that has been breached. With the hooves of his horses he will trample all your streets; he will slay your people by the sword, and your strong pillars will fall to the ground" (Ezekiel 26:3a, 9-11).

On the morning of September 11, 2001, I was on a plane from Los Angeles to Memphis. I had attended a business meeting the evening before. Now I was on my way to complete another. I sat in first class next to a tall, slender FedEx pilot. I thought nothing of it when the cockpit's pilot summoned the flight attendants. Everything seemed normal until one flight attendant—a tall, young blonde woman—emerged from the cockpit with a strange expression on her face. I knew something was wrong.

She tried to appear stoic, but as she passed, I saw her lower lip trembling. She was flushed from the neck up, and her eyes were wide puddles of tears. My heart stopped. There could be only one explanation.

I grabbed the arm of the FedEx pilot next to me and informed him in a panicked whisper, "I think we're going to crash!"

He and the two other FedEx pilots in first class already knew what was happening. He explained to me a plane had crashed into one of the Trade Towers in New York. A few minutes later, my FedEx friend, cell phone in hand, turned to me and whispered, "Another plane just crashed into the other Tower."

Finally, our pilot came over the PA system and announced we would have to make an emergency landing in Phoenix, Arizona. My immediate thought—*Memphis is nowhere near New York. Can't we make it to Memphis?* I do not know how reliable the FedEx pilot's information was, but he leaned over again and told me that we had 30 minutes to land, or our plane would be shot down.

"What? By whom?"

"The United States government."

Panicked out of my mind, I begged the Lord to let us land safely. I could not wait for the wheels to touch the tarmac. I was not ready for the chaos and confusion I saw in the airport terminal. Everyone was on the phone. Frenzied people swarmed in all directions. I called my office.

"WHAT IS GOING ON?" I yelled at my secretary, Claudia.

"Ray, we've been waiting for your call. All the staff is assembled in your office. Let me transfer you."

Claudia proceeded to explain what we all came to soon know. She booked me into a local hotel in Phoenix that became my home for the next six days. She also informed me people were calling because they remember me telling them something like this would happen. At first, I had no idea what she was talking about. Suddenly, I realized what was happening. I was now living the dreams the Lord had given me four years earlier!

Book Three: The Late Great United States

A Word of Caution

What is contained in these pages is not for everyone. Christ, the Head of the church, is calling His body, His bride out of the world and all of its trappings. He is coming back for a chaste spouse, one without spot or blemish.   He has given me many dreams in which His flawed, mottled companion has caused many to stumble.

When Christ walked the earth, He taught in parables. He still teaches in parables. He speaks and teaches in ways that are not direct, not black and white, but a heart filled with faith in Him can understand what His Spirit is saying.

The unbelieving heart cannot discern what the Spirit is saying. This book will be pure nonsense to nonbelievers. But for those who can hear God's Spirit, I will present to you what our Lord and Savior has revealed to me, in the order He revealed it. God's revelations to me were progressive. He did not share the big picture with me all at once. Instead, He revealed bits and pieces at different intervals, over many years, until the puzzle was complete.

I am not here to press my convictions on anyone. If your name is written in the Lamb's Book of Life, and God is calling you to come out of Babylon the Great, then you will understand the words written on these pages because God's Spirit will quicken your spirit.

I am not here to debate theology. Save your debates for when you see the Lord face to face. I cannot answer for Him. Perhaps, He will explain why He did things the way He did them. I will simply share the revelations He gave me over the years about the close of this age. It appears to commence with the economic collapse of the United States. The Lord and I have had many conversations about the age's end.

Yes, I hear the Lord's voice, and He hears mine. We talk back and forth. Mostly, He speaks to me in my spirit, although I have heard His audible voice. He communicates in complete sentences and whole paragraphs. Sometimes we talk all day. There have been times He has said nothing at all.

The Lord also speaks to me through His Word, through His Spirit, through my providential circumstances, through dreams and visions, through signs and wonders, through colors, through numbers, through names, through pain, and through people. You will see this as you review my journal entries. Why He chose me, I cannot tell you. That is one of the questions I have for Him when I see Him face to face.

Apparently, because this book has now been written, the Lord, in His manifold wisdom, unveiled things to me in a way that would bless others who were made privy to our talks. I never intended any portions of my journals to be released in my lifetime. Because they contain such sensitive material, I fully expected to be taken home to be with the Lord before anything was revealed. God had a different plan.

Only the Lord's Spirit can counsel and guide you on what you should do after you read this book. Since He has given you this information, I trust He has already gone before you to help you prepare wisely for what is coming. As you read, ask God to open your eyes, mind, and heart. Ask Him to speak to you about your life and the lives of your family members, friends, acquaintances, neighbors, and enemies. (Remember, we are to love our enemies too!) He will meet you wherever you are, whether you are a general in the faith or a newborn babe in Christ. Beloved, the Lord is with you.

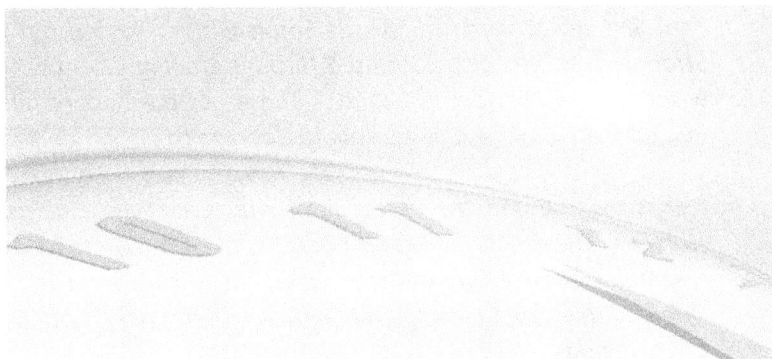

Chapter 1
Beware of the Hidden Culprit!

In the fall of 1994, God began to set the stage for my dreaming about His coming judgment on the United States. By this time, I had resigned from Burger King to form my own company, Inclusive Business Strategies (IBS)—a wealth-transfer ministry. I asked God to allow me to "transfer the wealth of the world into the kingdom of God for the salvation of souls in the last days." That was IBS's mission statement on paper. Shortly after crafting that statement, the Spirit of the Lord began to reveal things about riches that gave me second thoughts about our mission. The Lord encouraged me to proceed, but with great caution. He would use what He taught me to warn others.

November 15, 1994

The Deceitfulness of Riches

Riches can be a snare! More than ever before, I clearly see this. In Ezekiel 28, the king of Tyre is corrupted through commerce and trade. He becomes affluent, prosperous and begins to think he is a god. Wise in his own eyes, he is possessed by the spirits of pride and covetousness.

The next set of verses discusses Satan himself having too much. Strangely, he was also corrupted through trading. He was "full of wisdom" and "perfect in beauty." These got the best of him. He longed to be God. But he is brought down to the fiery depths.

Riches also caused the wisest man who ever lived, Solomon, to stumble. The excess sullied his heart. Look at the United States. It resembles ancient Tyre in many ways. Americans have too much. Our wealth corrupts us, and we think we do not need God. We are our own gods.

According to a recent U.S. study on charity giving—contrary to popular belief—those who have the least give the most. The nationwide study, conducted by the U.S. Internal Revenue Service, analyzed the tax returns of millions of Americans. Bottom line: Most affluent people hoard their wealth.

All this indicates riches can be a snare for human beings. We cannot handle it. No wonder the Word tells us, "It is hard for a rich man to enter the Kingdom of God." Only through the power of the Holy Spirit can a person who has great material wealth use it rightly for God's glory. Jesus also says, "There's nothing impossible for God." There are a few examples in the New Testament in which rich believers allow Christ to have His way with them—Lydia, Priscilla, and Aquila.

Years ago, God told me I would be tested by riches. He warned the test of prosperity was harder than the test of adversity. His counsel: "Use the wealth I give you for My glory. Manage it, knowing you must give Me an account in the end. It is a sharp test that few pass." God knows, I have struggled with covetousness for years. Repeatedly, Satan has tried to take me out of the race with this sin. I must stay on my guard.

At this point, God revealed to me there was something about trade and commerce—conducting and transacting business—that could be very harmful to the human spirit. Trade creates wealth, and left unchecked by His Spirit, riches can devour a person. Excessive wealth corrupts excessively, He warned. But there was more. The very *process* by which people achieved wealth had the capacity to make them proud and wise in their own eyes. Their heart attitude shouts: "Look at what I've done, what I've created, what I've accomplished!" Our posture should always be, "Look at what God is doing!"

Considering these truths, I concluded IBS's mission to transfer the wealth of the world into God's Kingdom would be a risky undertaking. I would be playing with fire. But God plainly told me, "The flames shall not set you ablaze."

Chapter 2
A Dreamer in Training

I dreamt my first dream ever on March 20, 1996. I was 42 years old and into Day Four of a "40-days" fast. That is, I was fasting in three and four-day segments, as my busy schedule allowed, until I reached 40 days as opposed to fasting 40 consecutive days. I was brand new to the dream business when God began to give me revelations about judging the United States.

At first, I was reluctant to attribute my dreams to God. They could have been from the enemy. But why would Satan warn God's people to come out of evil? Maybe, I ate too much pizza the night before. But why would the dreams make such sense and always be tied to something in the physical, temporal realm, like Scripture, to confirm their truth?

God, in His wisdom, gave me *a lot* of other dreams about ordinary, mundane things that came to pass. By repeatedly showing me people before I met them or events before they occurred, I came to understand in time, God was allowing me to glimpse the future in dreams.

Scenes from movies I had not yet seen would play out in my dreams. Sometimes, I would play an active role in a scene. Sometimes, I was just a spectator.

Once, in a dream I was trapped under mounds of debris and concrete. Barely able to breathe, I grew faint from claustrophobia. Two nights later, I saw a television documentary about an earthquake. In one scene, I saw a person trapped under mounds of fallen concrete and debris.

The commentator described to viewers what it felt like to be entombed in rubble. He spoke about the difficulty of breathing unless one found an air pocket. He also explained how some victims can become overwhelmed with claustrophobic feelings.

9/11

Occasionally, I saw visions of airplanes flying into buildings. I saw the crashes close, from different angles. However, I could never find a newspaper account to substantiate an airplane crashing into a building anywhere in the U.S. or Europe. There was a reason. The Lord gave me the dreams years before the 9/11 attack on the Trade Towers. Eventually, I stopped searching the papers.

In one dream, I distinctly remember seeing a woman with shoulder length black hair, dressed in a long-sleeve blouse and pleated skirt. She was on a high floor inside a building. She saw the jetliner coming toward her.

Suddenly, I morphed into the woman. (This happens often in my dreams. I take on an active role.) Now, I had her view. I had no fear because my mind simply could not grasp in that split second what was happening. The dream ended just before the plane hit.

When the Lord first began to give me dreams, I often took things literally when He meant them to be symbolic or metaphoric. Since I never found a news report of an airplane colliding into a building, I questioned if what I witnessed was the prophetic warning of an *actual* plane crash or was the crash *symbolic* of something else? Gradually, I became convinced it was symbolic. I was wrong.

Dreams Portending 9/11

On September 27, 1997, the Lord began to speak to me about His coming judgment on the United States. He spoke to me in a long, vivid parabolic dream. He spoke to me again, two days later, in another parabolic dream. Together, the dreams portended the 9/11 crisis. At the time, I did not realize it.

God gave me *two* dreams to confirm His judgment on the United States was a certainty. In Scripture, Joseph told Pharaoh the Lord had given the leader *two* dreams of a coming seven-year famine because the famine was a sure thing. It would absolutely come to pass. God requires at least *two* witnesses to confirm a matter (Deuteronomy 19:15, 2 Corinthians 13:1b).

September 27, 1997
A Dream: A Harried Mother and Two Sisters

Yesterday, I dreamt a strange dream. Upon awaking, I suspect it carried a spiritual message. I was absolutely convinced of it during my quiet time with the Lord, when I began to read my Bible passages for the day.

Unlike previous dreams, God did not give me instant understanding. I inquired of its meaning all day yesterday and the better part of today. During my time alone with Him this morning, He gave me some understanding of the dream's significance. When I went for my afternoon walk with Him, He flooded my being with understanding.

Book Three: The Late Great United States

A Harried Mother

The dream opened with an attractive, harried mother trying to take care of her household. She was busy in the kitchen when the dream began. She had many cares and I pitied her. The woman stumbled through her home trying to take care of this and that matter but failed at everything. She appeared disoriented. She married a useless husband. She pined that he never once stirred from the sofa to help her. He just laid there.

A striking aspect of the dream was that the woman had an abundance of food. In fact, she had too much. At one point, I chastised her. I asked, "Why did you prepare all of that when we have all of this?" She looked at me perplexed and shrugged her shoulders as if to say, "Why not?"

I followed behind her, trying to help her as she ran to and fro, accomplishing nothing. I tried to coax her to sit down, rest, and calm herself. I could bring her no comfort. She would not listen. The scene changed.

Two Sisters

Two sisters were going down an escalator. (The direction is very significant—not good!) One sister, the one in the back, appeared as though she had been shopping all day. Her arms were filled with packages. The sister in front had nothing. The sister in the back told the one in front that she had been doing some research and had made a startling discovery. "Silver is a lot better than gold," she announced. (She was covered in silver jewelry.) Her sister was unmistakably dubious.

"Let me tell you something," she warned. "You better make sure you know what you're doing, because there were many times I wanted to do things, and I rationalized 'like hell' to do them. I discovered too late I was wrong." The dream ended.

The fact that I remembered the dream so clearly, and it lingered long after I woke up, suggested it was significant. I finished my morning prayers. Then I opened my Bible to Ezekiel 22, where I left off the day before. The passage was about "the smelting furnace of judgment." In that chapter, God cataloged Israel's sins against Him:

See how each of the princes of Israel who are in you uses his power to shed blood. In you they have treated father and mother with contempt; in you they have oppressed the alien and mistreated the fatherless and the widow. You have despised My holy things and desecrated my Sabbaths. In you are slanderous men bent on shedding blood; in you are those who eat at the mountain shrines and commit lewd acts. In you are those who dishonor their fathers' bed, in you are those who violate women during their period, when they are ceremonially unclean. In you one man commits a detestable offense with his neighbor's wife, and another shamefully defiles his daughter-in-law, and another violates his sister, his own father's daughter. In you men accept bribes to shed blood; you take usury and excessive interest and make unjust gain from your neighbors by extortion. And you have forgotten Me, declares the Sovereign Lord (vv. 6-12, NIV).

The next set of verses reveal the certainty of her judgment for these sins. God told the prophet, "Son of man, the house of Israel has become dross to Me; all of them are the copper, tin, iron, and lead left inside a furnace. They are but the dross of silver" (Ezekiel 22:17-18, NIV). The word silver jumped off the page.

Therefore, this is what the Sovereign Lord says: "Because you have all become dross, I will gather you into Jerusalem. As men gather silver, copper, iron, lead, and tin into a furnace to melt it with a fiery blast, so will I gather you in my anger and my wrath and put you inside the city and melt you. I will gather you and I will blow on you with my fiery wrath, and you will be melted inside her. As silver is melted in a furnace, so you will

be melted inside her, and you will know that I the Lord have
poured out my wrath upon you" (vv. 19-22, NIV).

I dreamt about the topic of silver, never having done so before, and here silver was being discussed in my Bible passages for the day. When I next read Ezekiel 23, I became convinced God was speaking to me. It talked about the parable of two sisters! *Son of man, there were two women, daughters of the same mother. They became prostitutes in Egypt, engaging in prostitution from their youth (Ezekiel 23:2-3, NIV).*

The two sisters were Oholah and Oholibah. Oholah was Samaria, representing the Northern kingdom of Israel and Oholibah was Jerusalem, representing the Southern kingdom of Judah. Israel had been separated into northern and southern territories after Solomon's death. The king's descent into idolatry instigated the split.

Israel was the apple of God's eye. God had bestowed upon Israel a "priestly nation" status. She was to represent Him, the One True Sovereign God, to all the pagan nations of the world. Instead, she fell into idolatry and became like the nations around her.

Like a proud Husband, God had given her everything. Now He was angry. Both kingdoms had been unfaithful to Him. Verses 5-21 revealed their infidelities. Neither kingdom worshipped or trusted God any longer. They had been defiled by generations of idol worship. Rather than rely on God, they also sought protective alliances with Egypt and other nations. God likened them to prostitutes.

By the time of Ezekiel, God had already judged the older sister, the Northern kingdom. She had been conquered and scattered by the Assyrians. The younger sister had been repeatedly warned that she would suffer the same fate if she did not change. She refused to repent. She continued to exchange the Lord, her Husband, for other "lovers."

God warned that Babylon would invade Jerusalem and eventually destroy the Southern kingdom. Her judgment was now imminent:

> *... I am about to hand you over to those you hate, to those you turned away from in disgust. They will deal with you in hatred and take away everything you have worked for. They will leave you naked and bare, and the shame of your prostitution will be exposed. Your lewdness and promiscuity have brought this upon you, because you lusted after the nations and defiled yourself with their idols. You have gone the way of your sister; so I put her cup into your hand (Ezekiel 23:28-31, NIV).*

It was not until I read the morning newspaper, did I make the clear tie between the United States and ancient Israel! Israel's infidelities were the same ones committed daily in America—a so-called Christian nation. The newspaper headlines confirmed this truth. The margins of my Bible were covered with notations I had made throughout the years about the striking parallels between America and ancient Israel.

In my dream, the attractive, over-indulgent, harried, disoriented mother is the United States! Having fallen away from God, she is blind to her sins and stumbles in broad daylight. She is slowly unraveling and accomplishes nothing. Her house is falling apart. She is under God's judgment.

The husband in the dream, who never stirred from the couch, represents the idols ("lovers"), the woman has chosen for herself over God. These idols are useless, worthless. Yet, she exchanged God for them. Unlike God, they can do nothing for her. She laments this but does not know how to change her situation or fix the problem. God is the answer, but she is too blind to see this.

I represent the Church in the dream. I attempt to show the unhappy woman the way, but she would not stop long enough to listen. I could not comfort her. She was too consumed by her cares and worries to accept counsel.

God's judgment on America, the mother, is a certainty. America will go the way of the two sisters—the Northern kingdom of Israel and the Southern kingdom of Judah. America, like Israel, has lost her "priestly nation" status because she has strayed far from her Judeo-Christian roots and turned her back on God. Like the two sisters, God has given her everything.

America's abundance astounds the world. But like the two sisters, she has become a prostitute. In my dream, the older sister, who has already been judged and has nothing, tries to warn the younger sister. Successful and prosperous, the younger sister does not listen. She will eventually suffer her sister's fate. Judah (younger sister) was subjugated by the Babylonians just as Israel (older sister) was conquered earlier by the Assyrians.

Once flourishing and booming, America now is unraveling at the seams. Like the younger sister, she will not listen. America no longer loves the Lord. She has forgotten Him. His judgment will surely come upon her.

Just two days after the dream about the mother and two sisters, God gave me another. This time the dream was about modern-day traders.

September 29, 1997

Beware of the Spirit of Tyre!

Last night, I had another vivid dream. I surmised it was from the Lord, because, once again, it was so full of details. I am learning to sense when a dream is from God. Typically, they are rich in details, all of which I can fully remember upon awaking. God also seems to fill my being with understanding after the dream. Or, He points me to supporting passages of Scripture. The odds of me simply dreaming about a specific thing and then reading about it in Scripture are too astronomical to be by chance.

A Dream: Modern-Day Traders

In the dream, I entered a room full of executives. They were the top leaders of a company. A few were women, but most were men. They were from all different races and ethnic backgrounds. The meeting was about to start. We were told to take our seats. I realized the company was one I used to work for, Grand Metropolitan, PLC (also called GrandMet).

The conglomerate, headquartered in England, is not known for growing companies. It is known as a trader in the international business world. That means, it buys and sells companies (or brands) on a worldwide basis purely for profit.

GrandMet seeks to acquire companies with high-profile brand names. Then after running the acquisitions for a while, it breaks the companies into their component pieces and sells the parts to interested investors for a handsome profit. Selling the parts is more profitable than operating the company, at least in the short term. Of course, hundreds—even thousands—of employees are displaced in the process.

The world leader in the production and distribution of alcoholic beverages, GrandMet, at one point, had widespread interests in gambling casinos and was an investor in South Africa's apartheid system. It is ruthless in its business dealings. I know from first-hand experience. In this dream, the company served as a symbol of corrupt trade and commerce.

In the dream, we waited for the chairman and two other senior executives to arrive. They never came. We started the meeting without them. I took a seat in the back. A conductor took center stage. Apparently, they were going to start the meeting with music. A full orchestra sat in front of the conductor. The music started, and he began to lead us all in a blasphemous song: "Repeat after me! Altogether now: 'We are like gods! We are like gods!'"

I looked at the young woman sitting next to me. She had tears in her eyes. In my dream, she was a famous personality. I said, "That's it, I quit! I've had enough! I'm out of here!" I grabbed my things from underneath my chair and headed for the door. I warned her, "If you're tired of all this, then you should tell them so and leave." She did nothing. I left the room alone.

As I tried to exit the building, I was repeatedly beckoned by vendors selling their wares. A foreign vendor entreated me to try his exotic offering. The fare was so odd looking I could not make out what it was. After a few seconds, I realized it was some type of delicacy. I shook my head and went on my way. The dream ended.

I suspected my dream was from God, but I was not certain. I prayed and then opened my Bible to Ezekiel 26, the chapter where I had left off the preceding day. In that chapter, the Lord told Ezekiel to speak judgment against Tyre.

Tyre was a famous ancient, merchant city. Situated by the sea, Tyre traded extensively with many nations of the world. Through extensive commerce and trade, Tyre grew into a powerful, wealthy empire. It became too great for its own good. The Lord grew weary of Tyre's pride and greed and sent many nations against it, beginning with the king of the north—Nebuchadnezzar of Babylon:

The hoofs of his horses will trample all your streets; he will kill your people with the sword, and your strong pillars will fall to the ground. They will plunder your wealth and loot your merchandise; they will break down your walls and demolish your fine houses and throw your stones, timber and rubble into the sea. I will put an end to your noisy songs and music, and the music of your harps will be heard no more (Ezekiel 26:11-13, NIV).

The mention of songs and music caught my attention. In Ezekiel 27, the Lord instructed the prophet to "take up a lament concerning Tyre." In his lament, Ezekiel identified the many nations that traded with the great gateway city and what they traded. It was reminiscent of how America trades today with other nations of the world:

- *Men of Persia, Lydia and Put served as soldiers in your army....*
- *Men of Arvad and Helech manned your walls on every side; men of Gammad were in your towers.*
- *Tarshish did business with you because of your great wealth of goods; they exchanged silver, iron, tin and lead for your merchandise.*
- *Greece, Tubal and Meshech traded with you; they exchanged slaves and articles of bronze for your wares.*
- *Men of Beth Togarmah exchanged work horses, war horses and mules for your merchandise.*
- *The men of Rhodes traded with you, and many coastlands were your customers; they paid you with ivory tusks and ebony.*
- *Aram did business with you because of your many products; they exchanged turquoise, purple fabric, embroidered work, fine linen, coral and rubies for your merchandise.*
- *Judah and Israel traded with you; they exchanged wheat from Minnith and confections, honey, oil and balm for your wares.*
- *Damascus, because of your many products and great wealth of goods, did business with you in wine from Helbon and wool from Zahar.*
- *Danites and Greeks from Uzal bought your merchandise; they exchanged wrought iron; cassia and calamus for your wares.*
- *Dedan traded in saddle blankets with you.*
- *Arabia and all the princes of Kedar were your customers; they did business with you in lambs, ram, and goats.*

- *The merchants of Sheba and Raamah traded with you; for your merchandise, they exchanged the finest of all kinds of spices and precious stones, and gold.*
- *Haran, Canneh and Eden and merchants of Sheba, Asshur and Kilmad traded with you. In your marketplace, they traded with you beautiful garments, blue fabric, embroidered work and multicolored rugs with cords twisted and tightly knotted (Ezekiel 27:10-24, NIV).*

In Chapter 28, Ezekiel pronounced judgment on the king of Tyre. God was not pleased with this leader. He fancied himself a god because he had grown so prosperous and eminent. Ezekiel prophesied his fall:

In the pride of your heart you say, "I am a god; I sit on the throne of a god in the heart of the seas." But you are a man and not a god, though you think you are as wise as a god. Are you wiser than Daniel? Is no secret hidden from you? By your wisdom and understanding you have gained wealth for yourself and amassed gold and silver in your treasuries. By your great skill in trading, you have increased your wealth, and because of your wealth your heart has grown proud.

Because you think you are wise, as wise as a god, I am going to bring foreigners against you, the most ruthless of nations; they will draw their swords against your beauty and wisdom and pierce your shining splendor. They will bring you down to the pit, and you will die a violent death in the heart of the seas. Will you then say, "I am a god," in the hands of those who slay you? You will die the death of the uncircumcised at the hands of foreigners (Ezekiel 28:1-10, NIV).

Several mentions of the word god caused me to pause. I had just dreamt about a group of business executives who sang about being gods. Confident of a tie, I knew God would show me more.

Satan and Tyre's king had considerably much in common. Both imagined themselves gods. They were proud and covetousness. Just as God destroyed the king of Tyre because of his pride and arrogance, Satan will similarly be destroyed.

The next set of verses discussed Satan's fall, the reason he was booted from heaven. It spoke of his pending destruction. In the beginning, he was "the model of perfection, full of wisdom and perfect in beauty" (verse 12). Then he became full of himself and engaged in dishonest trade.

> You were blameless in your ways from the day you were created till wickedness was found in you. Through your widespread trade, you were filled with violence, and you sinned. So I drove you in disgrace from the mount of God, and I expelled you, O guardian cherub, from among the fiery stones. Your heart became proud on account of your beauty, and you corrupted your wisdom because of your splendor. So I threw you to the earth; I made a spectacle of you before kings. By your many sins and dishonest trade, you have desecrated your sanctuaries .... (Ezekiel 28:15-18a, NIV).

Satan was kicked out of heaven because he grew egotistical and wanted to be worshipped as God. In fact, he wanted to be God! God warns us against pride. The king of Tyre failed to heed this warning. Like Satan, he became swollen with conceit and pride.

In the second dream, the Lord plainly conveyed to me the United States is a latter-day Tyre—a prosperous, arrogant merchant nation, trading with other nations of the world. The U.S., like Tyre, has been taken captive by pride, materialism, and self-indulgence. Lost in her excesses, she has lost her moral compass. She can no longer be considered a Christian nation, representing Truth to other nations.

In our modern global economy, the United States is a world-class trader. Our status in commerce and trade within the world marketplace is much like that of ancient Tyre. Tyre was a pagan nation. In our post-Christian state, so are we. Like Tyre, the spirit of covetousness and pride has taken the United States captive. God will judge America just as He judged Tyre, its king, and ultimately, Satan.

No other nation on earth has been blessed like the United States. Our free enterprise system is the envy of the world and has produced unrivaled abundance. In our affluence, we have turned our backs on God. We have forgotten that He is the source of our fortunes, not we ourselves.

Prosperous and proud, we have failed to use our blessings and bounty to show other nations that God has revealed Himself through His Son, Jesus Christ, and only by faith in Him can we truly know God. Instead, we have hoarded our riches and exported our decadence.

We have become our own gods. It is little wonder that we have lost our godly influence on the rest of the world. Witnessing the ungodly fruits of our spiritual hypocrisy, many nations of the world today, particularly Islamic ones, reject anything remotely Western. Like ancient Israel, we have squandered the high privilege of representing God to other nations. Adrift from God and His Biblical teachings and statutes for decades, we are now in a moral and spiritual free fall.

In the dream, I again represent the Church. The Church must say, "Enough!" She must come out from all America's decadence and paganism. We have been called to be a holy people unto the Lord, separate and distinct from the world. We must not continue to participate in our nation's wickedness, but take deliberate, intentional steps to extricate ourselves. When we do, there will be those who will try to lure us back with the world's delicacies. But we must resist.

Many Americans have everything the world says they should. But like the famous young woman in my dream, they are still unhappy. Incredibly, they do not wish to be freed from the world's trappings.

They will perish with the world as Lot's wife perished when God destroyed Sodom and Gomorrah. She just could not let go of the world's stuff. She lost her soul *and* the stuff.

The Lord equating the U.S. to Tyre shed light on another odd tidbit in my personal life. In summer 1997, He began calling me "daughter of Tyre." For the longest time, I did not understand why. He frequently warned, "Beware of the spirit of Tyre, daughter of Tyre." After the dream, I finally understood He was cautioning me against becoming like most of my fellow countrymen. I was especially susceptible to being swept up in pride, covetousness, and greed because I lived in the United States, a contemporary Tyre.

Chapter 3
Walking in Ezekiel's Shoes

Six months after God gave me the two judgment dreams, He gave me another, in which I was introduced to a precocious four-year-old girl named Ezekiel. I turned out to be the little girl! Through this dream, God let me know that my ministry to His people, in many ways, would mirror that of the Old Testament prophet, Ezekiel.

My father in the dream was from GrandMet, a man I used to work for in real life, Barry Gibbons. Barry, a citizen of the United Kingdom, became CEO and president of Burger King Corporation when GrandMet acquired the burger chain in a 1989 hostile takeover. After the conquest, I was made a company officer. I reported directly to Nigel Travis, the executive vice president of Human Resources, who reported to Barry.

March 8, 1998

"Hi, My Name is Ezekiel!"

As I pondered the Ezekiel dream further and studied the life of the Prophet Ezekiel, I realized with sudden clarity I was the precocious little girl in my dream! God's hand in, and use of, my life closely parallel how God used Ezekiel. Seven major features characterized God has given me:

1. *Ezekiel ministry was chocked full of powerful and mysterious visions. So is mine.*
2. *God gave Ezekiel many bold parables to explain what was to come. God speaks to me in parables all the time. They reveal what is to come.*
3. *God used mundane objects and day to day situations to serve as symbols or media for Ezekiel's prophetic revelations. He does the same with me.*
4. *Ezekiel's message was largely one of doom and judgment on his people. This has been the constant refrain in the messages God has given me about the U.S.*
5. *More than any other prophet, God required Ezekiel to identify personally with the prophetic word given to him. He acted out prophetic symbolism. Last year, God told me I was the symbol and sign of the bride to come. Since that revelation, I have been walking out this symbolism in my everyday life.*
6. *Ezekiel delivered a lengthy lament of judgment against the city of Tyre. God instructed me to do the same for the U.S., certainly a modern-day Tyre.*
7. *Ezekiel's recordings were carefully arranged and dated. The Book of Ezekiel contains more dates than any other prophetic book in the Bible. I have compiled journals—more than a thousand pages. They span 13 years. I have tried to record and date everything God has revealed.*

Soon after the Lord gave me the "Hi, My Name is Ezekiel" dream, He began referring to me as "Z"—short for Ezekiel. In 2005, He began to present "Zs" to me everywhere I walked. I came to realize that often when I saw a "Z" in private or public, the Lord was trying to convey a message to me through it.

A few weeks after giving me the Ezekiel dream, the Lord began to pour into me more revelations about the early city of Tyre, which he commanded Ezekiel to speak a lament against. As "Z", would I have to do the same in my generation? What were God's specific issues with the United States that made it so much like the old merchant city of Tyre?

March 24, 1998

More Revelations on Tyre-U.S. Tie

I spent a good portion of my quiet time this morning meditating on the city of Tyre and its connection to the United States. Dating back as far as 1994, God told me the United States was a materialistic nation, and it would be severely judged in the future. Until I read the morning newspaper, I did not know why God led me to study the links between Tyre and the U.S. today. I saw more evidence of a nation in the grip of greed. One news article made God's point for Him.

The newspaper featured a national poll, conducted by USA Today/CNN/Gallup. The poll found that 69 percent of Americans thought President Clinton's moral standards were lower than their own. More than 60 percent thought he was dishonest and untrustworthy. However, 66 percent approved of the job he was doing as President.

Clinton's strong approval rating was largely because of the robust economy. Sixty-six percent rated the economy good to excellent, and a whopping 71 percent expected to be economically better off a year from now. (Our economy is at a 22-year high!)

Not surprisingly, 61 percent said they wanted the investigation into the Clinton sex scandal stopped. The polled suggested that even if Clinton were found guilty of sexual harassment and obstruction of justice, most Americans did not want him removed as President. Only 37 percent thought he should be impeached if the worst charges proved to be true. It is abundantly clear from the poll who is America's God: MONEY!

I was momentarily stunned. Then the connection hit me. What would one expect from the people of Tyre? Mammon ruled that empire. Mammon rules ours, not God.

The United States' free enterprise system has built the country into a global leader of commerce and trade. However, in our pursuit of worldly treasure, we have forgotten God. We have grown arrogant and proud just like the people of Tyre. God judged Tyre, and He will judge the United States.

God cautions that we cannot serve two masters (Matthew 6:24, Luke 16:13). He warns that we cannot serve Him *and* mammon. We must choose between the two, because, inevitability, we will end up serving one and despising the other.

According to the poll, mammon was America's clear choice. Despite all God instructs on the sins of lying, adultery, and abuse of power (pride), most Americans turned a blind eye to Clinton's sin because the country was prosperous. It was only a matter of time before we were completely undone as a nation.

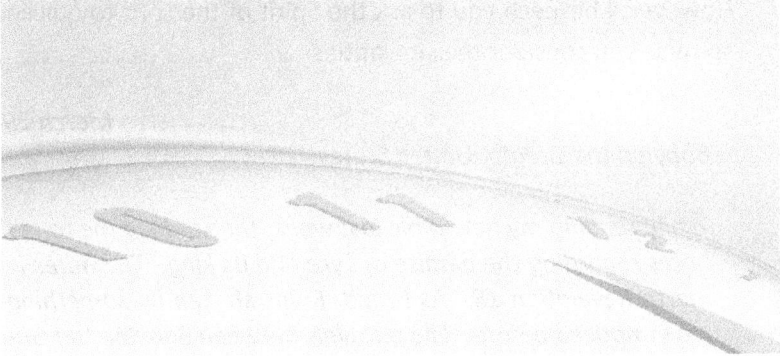

Chapter 4
United States = Babylon the Great!

Just five days after revealing the U.S. was like the merchant city of Tyre, the Lord floored me with another revelation. He linked Tyre to Babylon the Great—the corrupt city-nation spoken of by the Apostle John in the Book of Revelation. Then, He tied Babylon the Great to the United States! I recorded my insights and shared them with Jeri, my best friend, who shared them with a woman considered a biblical scholar at her church.

The woman became quite angry as she read my journal. She argued Babylon the Great was modern-day Iraq. Iraq, indeed, is the *physical* location of ancient Babylon, but we are not talking about matters of the temporal realm. While exiled on the Island of Patmos, God revealed to John a *spiritual* mystery—the destruction of a great commerce system at the end of the age. Its ruin would have grave implications for the entire world. The destruction of Iraq, then and now, would not have a devastating global impact.

Chances are many readers will have the same reaction as the woman when they see the United States associated with Babylon the Great. Many blood-bought followers of Jesus Christ will be troubled by this.

However, I beseech you to ask the Spirit of the Lord to quicken your spirit as you consider the similarities.

March 29, 1998

Babylon the Great = United States!!??

While reading my new Bible last week, the Lord led me to review its notes regarding the demise of Tyre and its king. The notes referred me to Revelation 18. As I read, I was shaken by something that I never noticed before. The parallels between Babylon the Great and Tyre were striking, absolutely striking!

God had already shown me an iron-clad tie between Tyre and the United States. The Bible commentary read: "Babylon the Great is the world's commercial system that will be destroyed by the Antichrist during the Great Tribulation." Could this not be the United States? Destroy the U.S., and the world's commercial-trade system, as we know it, would become extinct.

Some believe Babylon the Great represents a literal city, nation, or empire—a great one. The United States is such an empire. For whatever reason, I never linked Babylon the Great's obliteration to the America's destruction until now!

The Bible gives many clues to help identify or recognize Babylon the Great. God likens her to a wanton woman, a prostitute because she enticed the nations of the world to participate in her godless adulteries (idolatries).

The woman lured others, not by a newfangled, seductive religious philosophy or ideology. (That would come later when Babylon the Great joined with the apostate church during the Great Tribulation.) She beguiled the world to participate in her corruption through commercial trade! The nations of the world grew rich and corrupt by trading with her: "... *and the merchants of the earth grew rich from her excessive luxuries ... Your merchants were the world's great men.*

By your magic spell all the nations were led astray" (Revelation 18:3b, 23b, NIV).

For the first time, the United States started to take shape in my mind as the Great Whore. As a business executive in Corporate America for 23 years at that point, I had worked for and consulted with global companies. I held global positions and had a worldwide view of commerce and trade. I knew firsthand the kinds of activities that took place in business daily, and I was clear where the United States ranked in world trade—at the very pinnacle.

Following are 10 markers that identity Babylon the Great, a great commercial empire that will be destroyed at the end of the age, just before Christ's Second Coming. Its destruction will change commercial trade worldwide:

Clue #1: Unprecedented Abundance

No other nation on the face of the earth has benefited from the bounty the United States has enjoyed! Our free enterprise system has produced unprecedented abundance and has made us a world-class leader in trade. We are the envy of other nations.

The purchasing power of minority groups alone in the U.S.—more than one trillion dollars annually—rivals the domestic gross national products of entire nations such as the United Kingdom, Spain, Italy, Canada, and Australia.

The United States represents less than 5 percent of the world's peoples, but her citizens consume 30 percent of the world's resources! This is an astounding imbalance. The Bible tells us that God's judgment on Babylon the Great will equal the glory and luxury she lavished on herself. *"Give her as much torture and grief as the glory and luxury she gave herself"* (Revelation 18:7a, NIV).

Book Three: The Late Great United States

Clue #2: Arrogant and Proud from Wealth

In our wealth and prosperity, we have grown greedy, covetous, and proud. In the process of accumulating possessions, we have forgotten God. Not only have we forsaken His truths, we no longer see God as the Source of our abundance. The "spirit of Tyre" has taken us captive as a nation.

In our arrogance and pride, we have become our own gods (See Ezekiel 27). We see ourselves as the greatest, most powerful nation on earth, in a league of our own. Interestingly, the wealth and prosperity of Babylon the Great made her proud, boastful, and arrogant. *"In her heart she boasts, 'I sit as queen; I am not a widow, and I will never mourn'"* (Revelation 18:7b, NIV).

Clue #3: Coastal Merchant Empire

Babylon the Great—like Tyre—represents a renowned coastal merchant empire. So does the United States. All three nations are located on or near great bodies of water. This natural resource facilitated these nations becoming world class traders, importers and exporters of the world's goods.

Tyre was situated north of Jerusalem, off the Mediterranean Sea. This allowed Tyre to trade with many nations (see Ezekiel 27). The United States sits off two great oceans of the world—the Pacific Ocean on the west and the Atlantic Ocean on the east. The Gulf of Mexico graces the country's southeastern region. We learned from those who lament Babylon the Great's destruction that, she too, is a great merchant nation, positioned near coastal waters:

Every sea captain, and all who travel by ship, the sailors, and all who earn their living from the sea, will stand far off. When they see the smoke of her burning, they will exclaim, "Was there ever a city like this great city?" They will throw dust on their heads, and with weeping and mourning, cry out: "Woe! Woe, O great city, where all who had ships on the sea became rich through her wealth! In one hour, she has been brought to ruin!" (Revelation 18:17b-19, NIV)

Clue #4: Mammon Rules, Not God

Babylon the Great is called the Great Prostitute. Forsaking what is true and right, she prostitutes herself by piling up great wealth to the injury of herself and others. Mammon is her god.

In America's post-Christian state, Cash is King, not Christ. This was proven years ago, by the findings of a national poll, in which the majority of Americans did not want then President Clinton impeached for a sex scandal because of the strong economy. (See Chapter 3, p. 29).

Clue #5: Mistreats the Saints of God

In America's post-Christian state, believers in Christ are a persecuted minority. Referred to as the lunatic fringe or radical right, they are often ridiculed by popular culture and the media for their stance on abortion, gay and lesbianism, mercy killings, and other issues. Frequently, the Christian faith is undermined and maligned in movies and television, and Christians continue to be the butt of popular jokes within the American culture.

Prayer has been taken out of the nation's public schools, and the Ten Commandments have been removed from municipal government buildings nationwide. Some politicians have even tried to revoke the non-profit, charitable status of churches. The U.S. government continues to pass and uphold godless legislation. The list goes on. Persecution of God's people within U.S. borders will reach sinister heights during the Great Tribulation.

Interestingly, Babylon the Great disdains and mistreats the saints of God so much that God exhorts His people to rejoice at her demise: *"Rejoice over her, O heaven! Rejoice, saints and apostles and prophets!   God has judged her for the way she treated you"* *(Revelation 18:20, NIV).*

Clue #6: Lures Other Nations

Babylon the Great entices the nations of world to participate in her infidelities. She seduces them to join in her fornications. *"For all the nations have drunk the maddening wine of her adulteries. The kings of the earth committed adultery with her ...." (Revelation 18:3a, NIV).*

Having abandoned her Judeo-Christian roots, the United States failed to use her wealth to show other nations that God has revealed Himself through His Son, Jesus Christ. Instead, we have hoarded our wealth and exported our decadence. For example, the United States is the world's largest producer of pornography. Our lewd and obscene movies are translated into languages across the globe. And now we have taken our smut to international cyberspace.

In the meantime, the world is in desperate, dire need of a Savior to rescue it from its deplorable spiritual and physical conditions. In the face of all of this, ponder this stunning statistic: According to a study by Cru (formerly Campus Crusade for Christ), 80 percent of wealth needed to evangelize the remainder of the world is held by American Christians! This is an awful indictment on the American Church.

Clue #7: God's People Lulled to Sleep by Riches

God orders His people to come out of Babylon the Great. Apparently, they unwittingly become entangled in its commercial idolatries; they are deceived by riches along with the rest of the world. He strongly warns them to come out and not to participate in her unfaithfulness toward Him. *"Come out of her, my people, so that you will not share in her sins, so that you will not receive any of her plagues; for her sins are piled up to heaven, and God has remembered her crimes"* (Revelation 18:4-5, NIV).

The American church is lukewarm, at best. Complacent, she aptly fits the description of the church of Laodicea: *"You say, 'I am rich, I have acquired wealth and do not need a thing.' But you do not realize that you are wretched, pitiful, poor, blind and naked"* (Revelation 3:17, NIV).

If I were Satan, and I knew the vast majority of wealth to evangelize the world concentrated in a single nation, I would do everything in my power to persuade God's people to squander their riches on temporal things. This is precisely what has happened in the American church. She is asleep. God will vomit her out of His mouth if she does not wake up soon and repent.

Clue #8: Destroyed by Nuclear Missiles?

How will God judge Babylon the Great? It sounds eerily like a nuclear holocaust. *"Therefore, in one day her plagues will overtake her; death, mourning, and famine. She will be consumed by fire, for mighty is the Lord God who judges her...."* (Revelation 18:8, NIV). Scripture informs us that in a single day, in one hour Babylon the Great will be destroyed by fire (Revelation 18:9, 19). How does one destroy a commercial world system by fire?

If the nucleus of the world's commercial trade structure rests within a specific nation, then when that nation is destroyed, world trade, as we know it, would be demolished. Surely, a city or nation can be destroyed in a single hour, by a nuclear blast. The result of this holocaust will be death. Mourning, famine, and disease follow those who survive.

The likelihood of the United States being destroyed by a nuclear missile is not at all improbable. The CIA reports that many third world countries today have such nuclear capability since the breakup of the USSR. The Bible reveals Satan will be behind this destruction, using the Antichrist to destroy Babylon the Great (Revelation 17:12, 16-17).

Clue #9: The World's Reaction

Imagine for a second if the United States of America was suddenly wiped off the world map. How do you think the world would react? Would it not be as follows?

> *When the kings of the earth who committed adultery with her and shared her luxury see the smoke of her burning, they will weep and mourn over her. Terrified at her torment, they will stand far off and cry: "Woe! Woe, O great city, O Babylon, city of power! In one hour, your doom has come!" The merchants of the earth will weep and mourn over her because no one buys their cargoes any more— cargoes of gold, silver, precious stones, and pearls; fine linen, purple, silk and scarlet cloth; every sort of citron wood, and articles of every kind made of ivory, costly wood, bronze, iron and marble; cargoes of cinnamon and spice, of incense, myrrh and frankincense, of wine and olive oil, of fine flour and wheat; cattle and sheep; horses and carriages; and bodies and souls of men (Revelation 18:9-13, NIV).*

They will say, *"The fruit you longed for is gone from you. All your riches and splendor have vanished, never to be recovered."* The merchants who sold these things and gained their wealth from her will stand far off, terrified at her torment (Revelation 18:14-15, NIV). Would this not be the reaction of the world to the United States' demise? There is no question. It would be.

Clue #10: The Descriptive Name "Babylon" Fits

Why does God call the Great Prostitute, "Babylon the Great?" It is a meaningful and symbolic description of the empire. Babylon derives its name from the Babel, dating back to the Tower of Babel (Gen. 11). Since that time, Babylon has been a symbol of man's pride and rebellion against God.

Nimrod, who fancied himself a god, wanted to build a tower that would reach to the heavens to snub God. Against God's command to populate the entire earth, he attempted to build a great city-center, Babylonia. It would be a renowned empire. Such a place would lure the people of the world to settle there. Babylonia was also Nimrod's attempt, in defiance of God, to create a center for idolatry and sorcery.

Recognizing the people's fallen purposes, God confused their language so that they could no longer communicate with one another. This forced the people to separate and populate the earth as God had originally commanded. This event explains the diversity of languages in the world today.

Today, the United States is the most racially and ethnically diverse country on the face of the earth. Historically, it has been the melting pot for other nations, a land that offers liberty and religious freedom to the peoples of the world. America's participation in the Transatlantic Slave Trade also played a role in her racial diversity. Lastly, many foreigners dream of striking it rich in America. For this reason, people come from all over the world to settle in the U.S. They speak many different languages and dialects just as they did in the ancient city of Babel, after God confused their tongues.

In addition, the United States is no stranger to the occult, and will be entrenched in dark magic at the close of the age. Today, she has extensive ties to the occult and witchcraft simply by way of her broad acceptance and involvement in the practice of freemasonry. Many Christians are freemasons; they have no idea of its link to the occult. However, this is only the tip of the problem. Other secret society abominations have penetrated many communities and the highest levels of our government. The name Babylon is a fitting description of the United States as a renowned commercial world empire, comprised of the many different peoples of diverse languages, engulfed in sorcery and rebellion.

Chapter 5
April's Rapture Dreams

Saints Go Up as Fire Falls

Just two months after God deposited into my spirit that the United States was the Great Whore (Babylon the Great), He gave a member of my staff at Denny's, April Kelly, a relatively new believer in Christ, a horrifying, but revelatory dream. She relayed it to me.

In the dream, the worldwide rapture occurs as fire falls from the sky. The saints of God, symbolized by sheep, are caught up and removed from earth at or around this time.

The fire's source is not clear from the dream. For years, I thought the fire was the result of nuclear blasts and confined to the United States. This still may be true. But more recently, I have come to suspect the fire is a heavenly firestorm and its destruction is worldwide. The fire may be connected to the breaking of the Sixth Seal. Per Revelation 6:12-17, the breaking of this seal commences the Day of the Lord. It is when God rises to judge *all* rebellion on earth and in heaven. It results in the expulsion of Satan and his cohorts from heaven. They are cast to earth. (See Chapter 20 for a fuller discussion of this event.)

Book Three: The Late Great United States

In April's dream, the rapture seems to occur at a time when there is a fight in heaven. Archangel Michael and his angels fight demonic forces. Christ suddenly enters the scene and ends it all. Satan and his minions are defeated and are presumably cast to earth. Beautiful, melodic singing in heaven follows Satan's defeat.

May 24, 1998

April's Dream: The Rapture and a War in Heaven

When Ryan and I returned from Michigan to South Carolina to pack up the house, I had five messages on my home-office voicemail. The last one was from April. She dreamt a frightening dream and insisted I call her the moment I received her message. The time did not matter. April had been taking a week's vacation. I called her immediately. I never heard her more excited. This is what she relayed:

Raining Fire on Earth

I was inside a house. Suddenly a bright light began to permeate the interior. Not only was the light coming through the windows, but also through the walls and roof. I was drawn to the light. I stepped outside and saw an incredible sight—sheep floating upward in the sky!

The sheep had been caught up in the light. People were watching on the ground, pointing at the sheep being pulled into and up by the light. I, along with two other persons, whom I did not know, were spectators of all this. I had complete peace.

As we moved, it was as if we were floating, not walking. We moved too quickly to be walking. Everywhere, people were running and screaming. The police and military troops with huge hoses sprayed water on the ground.

I asked what was going on. A man handed me a wet white sheet. "You will be safe with this on," he said. That's when I noticed it was raining fire! Fire was pouring from the sky!

I entered another house. Inside the house people were screaming and crying. They were trying to hide from the fire. Suddenly, someone noticed the fire burning through the roof! The people were in terror. Outside again, I saw fire burn the tires off cars as people tried to flee in them. The scene changed.

Satan's Defeat in Heaven

Now I was in a theater. I was sitting behind a dark figure who sat on a throne. Looking forward pass this dark figure, I saw angels coming toward it. The angels had swords. Suddenly, demons with horrid faces flew in front of the angels. A battle ensued. The dark figure never left his throne.

Then a Bright Light entered the room. The demons stopped fighting and fled the moment the Bright Light entered. The Figure of bright light wielded a sword. His countenance was so bright I could not see His face. He came right up to the dark figure and pierced him through with a sword. The dark figure gave a loud shriek.

A loud explosion followed. After the explosion, everything was quiet, peaceful. All I could hear was beautiful singing. The song I heard was heavenly—too beautiful to describe. My dream ended with the beautiful singing.

April stressed to me that she did not watch horror movies or read scary books. She explained that her life was too tame and uneventful to conjure up such a fantasy. The dream, lush in detail, came out of nowhere.

"It was like it was really happening!" she squealed. "It felt so real!" A relatively new believer in the Lord, I was aware April knew very little about end-time events as described in Scripture. Her dream was from the Lord.

There was no question in my mind, April dreamt about the rapture of the Church and the judgments that will befall nonbelievers and Satan and his demons near the close of the age. I could not tell from her dream if the fight in heaven and the rapture happened at the same time or if one preceded the other.

Eight months later, the Lord gave April another horrifying dream. Only this time, He revealed the geographic region impacted by the fiery rainstorm. In this dream, April saw the worldwide rapture occur as fire fell from the sky on the *United States*! It is conceivable that the firestorm occurred worldwide, but that God allowed April to see its impact on U.S. soil only.

We knew it was the U.S. because God included two well-known African Americans in the dream. Interestingly, the two leaders hold different philosophical views on how blacks should deal with racism. One says look to God for deliverance; the other says agitate and advocate for change. In the dream, each leader had a following.

In both dreams, God could not make it any clearer that the worldwide rapture will occur as fire rains from the sky. God has given me many dreams of the rapture. In those dreams, people disappear in an instant. One moment they are present and the next instant they are gone. I never see them disappear. According to Scripture, the rapture happens in a flash, in the twinkling of an eye (1 Corinthians 15:52). However, God allowed April to witness the rapture in her dreams to confirm it was actually happening.

October 19, 1998

April's Dream: Saints Safe During Judgment

Today, April relayed an extraordinary dream to Dora and me. She could not wait to tell us. When the dream began, she was with two friends—Sheila, a mutual acquaintance of ours, and Sheila's cousin

Junior. All three are believers in Christ. They were standing in front of a huge white door.

April knocked on the door. Much to her surprise, her grandmother, who died earlier this year, opened the door. April gave her a big hug. Busy wrapping wedding gifts, her grandmother invited them in. April described the wrapping paper as the most beautiful she had ever seen. Before they left, her grandmother warned them not to go near the border. As April shut the door behind her, she wondered ... what border?

April looked out over the horizon and saw the border. The three wandered toward it. Suddenly, Junior decided to cross over to see what was on the other side. The second he stepped over, he disappeared. Sheila, also curious, wanted to see what was on the other side. April reminded her of her grandmother's warning. It fell on deaf ears. Sheila jumped over and disappeared. Then April, against her better judgment, reluctantly stepped over too.

Instantly she found herself on earth. In every direction she said "homeless people" of all races and nationalities were running frantically. They did not have the appearance of regular homeless people; they simply had nowhere to go, nowhere to turn, nowhere to hide. She glanced to her left and saw two prominent figures from the African American community. Each was leading a group of black people.

Suddenly, a huge fireball appeared in the sky. A fiery cloud covered the entire sky. As it began to rain fire, people screamed and ran in terror. April was also terrified. Then a voice whispered in her ear, "Don't be afraid! You are a spirit!" Peace washed over her, banishing her fear.

She looked out over the sky. On the horizon, she saw Bibles rising toward heaven. Intermingled with the Bibles were white sheets of paper floating upwards. She glided to the rising papers and grabbed one. She saw the obituary of a woman she had not seen since she was a little girl. The woman is currently ill with cancer. Her dream ended.

After I heard April's dream, several thoughts occurred to me. I recorded them in my prayer journal:

1. The Bibles rising upward represent people who believe in Jesus Christ, the Word of God. At the time of the rapture, they are "alive in Christ."
2. The obituaries represent believers who have died in Christ. Their bodies are resurrected at the rapture as Scripture promises. They are caught up with those who are alive in Christ (1 Thessalonians 4:16-17).
3. Fire rains down on nonbelievers, those who refused eternal life through Jesus Christ. Believers are saved out of the fiery judgment. Nonbelievers are not.
4. The presence of two highly esteemed African Americans in the dream suggests there may be some type of racial crisis occurring in the U.S. when the fire falls. The Lord could have featured any number of leading Americans, but He chose those two for a reason.
5. While fiery judgments fall on earth, wedding preparations are being made in heaven. At this point, the bride of Christ is in heaven with Him. She is without spot, stain, or blemish. She will be presented to Him at The Wedding Feast of the Lamb.

Chapter 6
Is Babylon the Great Destroyed by Nuclear Blasts?

Several Scripture passages seem to indicate that Babylon the Great will be pummeled and extinguished by nuclear missiles, not by a heaven-sent firestorm. We know from Scripture that Babylon the Great is destroyed by fire, set ablaze by enemy nations. They are led by the Antichrist. Other nations that witness her demise, remain to see her ruin. The destruction happens on a single day within one hour:

- "Therefore, her plagues will come in *one day*—death and mourning and famine. And she will be utterly *burned with fire,* for strong is the Lord God who judges her" (Revelation 18:8, emphasis mine).
- "The ten horns which you saw are ten kings who have received no kingdom as yet, but they receive authority for *one hour* as kings with the beast … and the ten horns which you saw on the beast, these will hate the harlot, make her desolate and naked, eat her flesh and *burn her with fire*" (Revelation 17:12, 16, emphasis mine).

- "Alas, alas, that great city Babylon, that mighty city! For in *one hour* your judgment has come" (Revelation 18:10, emphasis mine).
- "For in *one hour* such great riches came to nothing. Every shipmaster, all who travel by ship, sailors, and as many as trade on the sea, stood at a distance and cried out when they saw the *smoke of her burning...*" (Revelation 18:17, emphasis mine).
- "Alas, alas, that great city, in which all who had ships on the sea became rich by her wealth! For in *one hour* she is made desolate" (Revelation 18:19, emphasis mine).

The Prophet Zechariah spoke extensively about the Day of the Lord, and what would happen to the nations that fought against Israel. In that day, he prophesied that God would destroy the enemies of Jerusalem in the following manner: "Their flesh shall dissolve while they stand on their feet, their eyes shall dissolve in their sockets, and their tongues shall dissolve in their mouths" (Zechariah 14:12). The sudden and complete disintegration of people may signal the employment of nuclear missiles.

In Jeremiah 51:25, Babylon is referred to as "a destroying mountain, who destroys all the earth," against whom God has stretched His hand. It is a layered passage of Scripture. It prophesied ancient Babylon's destruction by the Medes and Persians, but it also pointed to the latter-day fulfillment of Babylon the Great's ruin.

In that Scripture, God foretold through the Prophet Jeremiah that Babylon would be rolled down from the rocks—its high place—and made a burnt mountain. He promised no one would take "a stone for a corner nor a stone for a foundation" (v. 26). This may be because

Babylon the Great will be utterly destroyed without a stone left, or more likely, because of nuclear contamination.

The Lord has given me at least three dreams that seem to show the U.S. being destroyed by nuclear blasts. The first dream was in 1997. The second one occurred 11 years later in December 2008. Three months later, He gave me yet another.

A distinct feature in two of the dreams is that the blasts come from an eastern direction. Everything blows from east to west. Intriguingly, Tyre is broken in the midst of the seas by "an east wind." A synopsis of the three dreams is captured in the journal entry below.

May 9, 2009

Tyre Broken by "An East Wind"

While reading about Tyre's demise, Ezekiel spoke of an east wind destroying Tyre: "... but the east wind broke you in the midst of the seas" (Ezekiel 27:26). The verse is layered. In ancient times, Babylon was the east wind that broke Tyre. In modern times, Iraq (modern-day Babylon) and other Middle Eastern (Islamic) nations may represent the east wind that breaks the U.S.

God has given me two dreams in which I see a strong destructive wind that distinctly blows from east to west. The wind uproots and destroys my immediate surroundings. In both dreams, I witness the destruction of the U.S. by nuclear blasts, and in both dreams, I and others end up in heaven.

In yet another dream, I am standing in a room when suddenly all my surroundings disintegrate. They melt away right before my eyes. I look outside just in time to see the whole neighborhood disappear. It melts or drips away like wet paint running down a white canvas. In the last scene, I see insets of families across the world watching the meltdown from afar on televisions. Surely, these are nuclear blasts I am witnessing!

The day before I recorded the above journal entry about nuclear blasts hitting the U.S., God gave me two visions of policemen trying to quell civil unrest in the U.S. The timing of the visions was so close to my three nuclear blast dreams that it made me think the nation would be in the midst of some kind of internal conflict or turmoil when the missiles struck.

May 9, 2009

Two Visions—Civil Unrest in U.S.

I had two visions last night and I know they must do with civil unrest in the U.S. In the first vision, I saw sleek dogs running, chasing people. They were attack dogs unleashed on people. In the second vision of the night, I saw policemen riding on wide motorcycles. The policemen were sent to quell rioting. I have had other dreams in which I have seen Americans behind barb-wire fences. What could cause such civil unrest? Am I witnessing martial law on American soil?

The two visions of civil unrest in the U.S. reminded me of April's dream, in which she saw two prominent African Americans leading a group of black people. There is a hint in all this that the U.S. may be embroiled in racial conflict when destruction comes upon her unawares.

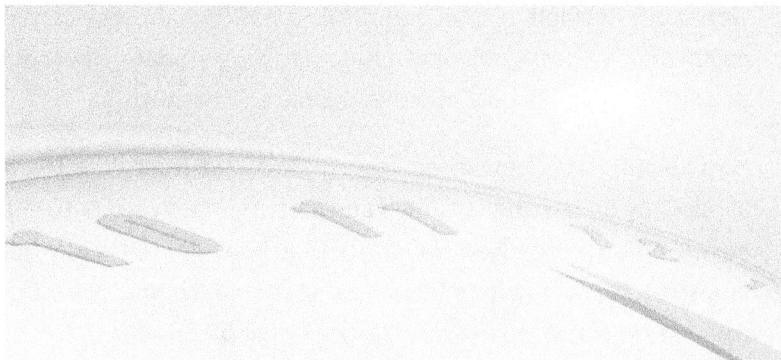

Chapter 7
Did Habakkuk Foretell Our Day of Doom?

God deals in shadows, types, and patterns. Frequently, events under the Old Covenant foreshadow a New Covenant *spiritual* reality. That is, an event that happened under the Old Covenant in the visible, temporal realm *before* Christ's appearance on the world stage, presages a future event that unfolds under the New Covenant. And, the future event often reveals a hidden spiritual truth.

For example, the Great Exodus led by Moses, delivered God's children from Egyptian bondage through a desert wilderness to the Promised Land, Canaan. That arduous 40-year trek foreshadowed the journey all followers of Christ will take after they are *spiritually* delivered from the bondage of this world. (In Scripture, the world is a type of Egypt.) God will test and prove their faith as they trudge through a long wilderness of trials and tribulation to His promises for their lives. Eventually, they will be delivered to the *ultimate* Promised Land— heaven! Thus, the rapture of the Church is the New Covenant fulfillment of the Great Exodus under the Old Covenant.

Looking at the Book of Habakkuk, God revealed to the prophet, a contemporary of Jeremiah, Ezekiel, Daniel, and Zephaniah, that He would use Babylon, a cruel and ruthless nation Habakkuk considered pagan and far "less godly" than Judah, to judge Judah. How could He do this? Judah was God's chosen people and heritage!

Notwithstanding her chosen status, God told Habakkuk He would allow Babylon to conquer Judah and carry her into slavery to chastise her. God also promised Habakkuk that Babylon, in time, would be punished for her wickedness, and particularly for her merciless, ruthless treatment of His people (Jeremiah 50:33-35). This came to pass when the Medes and Persians, in a single day, entered the great city by stealth and overthrew the hapless Babylonians, engaged in a drunken revelry.

Layered within the passages of this ancient book is the suggestion of the destruction of a latter-day Babylon—a Babylon whose works will be consumed by fire at a time when the Lord seeks "to fill the entire earth with the knowledge of Himself" (Habakkuk 2:13-14). If Habakkuk's prophecies foretell of a latter-day destruction of Babylon, which is clearly Babylon the Great, then we are given great insight into two things: who God will use to lead the U.S.'s destruction and His *real* underlying grievance with the nation.

Ancient Persians are Today's Iranians

It is a clear point of history that the Medo-Persian Empire sacked ancient Babylon. The descendants of ancient Persia are today's Iranians. Other prophetic pronouncements against Babylon by Jeremiah and the Apostle John suggest modern-day Iran may align with Russia and several other nations in the destruction of the U.S. It is important to note the *daughter* of Babylon, that is, an *offspring* of Mother Babylon, shall be destroyed by fire in just one hour. Nothing short of a nuclear explosion could accomplish such a feat:

Behold, a great people shall come from the north (Russia), a great nation and many kings shall be raised up from the ends of the earth. They shall hold the bow and the lance; they are cruel and shall not show mercy... set in array, like a man for the battle, against you, O daughter of Babylon (Jeremiah 50:41-42).

The ten horns which you saw are ten kings, who have received no kingdom as yet, but they receive authority for one hour as kings with the beast. ... And the ten horns which you saw on the beast, these will hate the harlot, make her desolate and naked, eat her flesh, and burn her with fire (Revelation 17:12, 16).

A Nation Built on Bloodshed ...

Habakkuk warned Babylon that it would pay for building its high nest with the blood of peoples from other nations:

Because you have plundered many nations, all the remnant of the people shall plunder you, because of men's blood and the violence of the land and the city, and all who dwell in it. Woe to him who covets evil gain for his house, that he may set his nest on high, that he may be delivered from the power of disaster! You give shameful counsel to your house, cutting off many peoples, and sin against your soul. For the stone will cry out from the wall, and the beam from timbers will answer it. Woe to him who builds a town with bloodshed, who establishes a city by iniquity (Habakkuk 2:8-12).

It is an indisputable fact of history that much of the United States was built on the backs of African slaves after the system of enslaving Native Americans failed. America's involvement in the African slave trade began in 1619, when 16 slaves arrived in Jamestown, Virginia. It lasted 246 years, after decimating millions upon millions of lives.

As discussed in Book Two, *Two Hidden Treasures*, many of today's African Americans are descendants of the lost tribes of Israel. They have Hebrew blood running through their veins. They are Ephraim—

Judah's brethren and God's heritage. Slavery in "Babylon" was punishment for their idolatry, just as it was for their forefathers! Millions of Jacob's descendants were mercilessly murdered to establish the great republic we know today as the United States of America. Thus, God's fundamental issue with the U.S. is its founding citizens, fueled by covetousness and greed, ruthlessly annihilated His heritage through a brutal slave system that lasted nearly 250 years.

The repercussions of America's participation in slavery can still be seen and felt throughout the country today, nearly 150 years later. Most African Americans continue to suffer under the stigmatism of racism in America. Race continues to divide the nation. Thus, Habakkuk's warning to the Babylon of his time echoes across the millennia to present-day citizens of the U.S.—Babylon the Great: *"Woe to him who builds a town with bloodshed, who establishes a city by iniquity"* (Habakkuk 2:12).

Also, through the Prophet Jeremiah, God promised destruction to the nations where He scattered His heritage: *"For I am with you, says the Lord, to save you; though I will make a full end of all nations where I have scattered you, yet I will not make a complete end of you"* (Jeremiah 30:11).

Dismantled by Debt

Habakkuk warned Babylon that covetousness and greed—the sins that set in motion the ripping of peoples from their homelands—would be the nation's undoing. Babylon "loaded itself up with many pledges" to the point that it could not repay. Obsessed with abundant and lavish living, Babylon not only plundered people of other nations, its greed put it at the mercy of unsympathetic creditors. Another warning quite appropriate for the great United States:

He is a proud man, and he does not stay at home. Because he enlarges his desire as hell, and he is like death, and cannot be satisfied, he gathers to himself all nations and heaps up for himself all peoples.... Woe to him who increases what is not his—how long? And to him who loads himself up with many pledges? Will not your creditors rise up suddenly? Will they not awaken who oppress you? And you will become their booty (Habakkuk 2:5, 7).

As of February 2013, the United States' national debt topped $16.7 trillion—a staggering debt that would take many generations to pay. Presently, the nation cannot afford to pay the interest on the debt, much less the principle. China, the largest investor in U.S. Treasuries, owns nearly one-quarter of the nation's overseas debt, which puts the U.S. in a precarious financial position should China stop buying U.S. bonds or sell off its position. Treasury prices would tumble, and yields would rise, negatively impacting the already vulnerable economy.

Japan, Brazil, Taiwan, Switzerland and more than 30 other foreign governments also hold stakes in U.S. bonds. Today, the United States is an unwitting slave to its foreign lenders (Proverbs 22:7).

Just as covetousness and greed played a large role in ancient Babylon's undoing, God will allow the same to dismantle Babylon the Great, before her destruction. The U.S. pillaged and plundered for profit. Now she will become her creditors' booty.

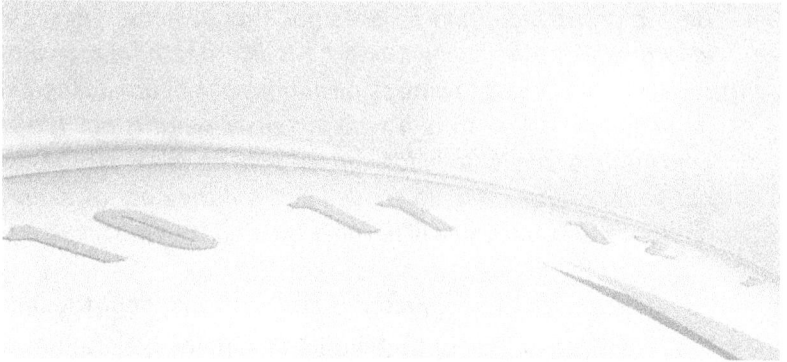

Chapter 8
A Titanic Connection

Years ago, the Lord began to talk to me about the connection between the sinking of the Titanic and the sinking of the United States, *literally.* Years later, I discovered I was not the only person to make the association. I heard sermons on it, and I read books about it. Since the Spirit of God is speaking to so many of us about it, we do well to heed the lessons learned from the sinking of the fated ship.

The U.S.—A Doomed Ship

God has given me several dreams about being on a doomed ship. In the dreams, the United States represents the condemned vessel. In a dream the Lord gave me on December 31, 2009, I had a suite of rooms on the ship that I wanted to show my friends. But for the life of me, I could not find it. I searched high and low. While I could not find my place on the lost boat, the spotted bride and her entourage, found theirs.

December 31, 2009

A Dream: No Room on the Ship

I had a strange dream this morning that I know is prophetic. In the dream, I saw a young woman who was getting married. She and her large wedding party were having difficulty boarding a big ship, where she was to be married. She was quite upset about it, causing a scene. I never saw the groom.

Suddenly, I found myself amid masses, trying to board the large ship. I did not know where the vessel was going. The two lines to board the boat were extraordinarily long. I waited my turn in line.

When I arrived on deck, I saw the bridesmaids from the wedding party. The women were standing in a large semicircle, dressed in white with white corsages pinned to their gowns. Then I saw the bride. She was dressed in a big white, flowing wedding gown. Although her gown was beautiful, her face was covered with big black spots!

Trying my best to ignore her spotted face, I said, "You made it after all?" She nodded. I gave her a hug and mumbled something about finding my place on the boat.

First, I entered a big empty room. I sat down and looked around. For the first time, I noticed the ship was quite worn, shabby even. Why hadn't I realized this before?

In the next scene, I wanted to show a group of friends the suite of rooms (or offices) I used to occupy on the ship. It was as though I used to live or work on the boat before. I searched up and down the ship, but I could not find my old space.

"I know it's here somewhere," I assured them. "Let's walk a little farther. I'll show you. It's probably just around this corner. Okay,

maybe it's around the next corner. Just wait. We'll come to it." On and on I went. I never found my place.

Suddenly, I realized I did not have my book. I had been reading a great book and I felt I simply had to have it on the trip. I shot off the boat.

Outside, I noticed nearly everyone who was going had boarded the ship. The lines outside were gone. I told the people in charge I would be back in less than five minutes. As I ran toward a building, where I last saw my book, I spotted a crumpled dollar bill. I snatched it up, crammed it into my pocket and kept running.

Once inside the building, I searched room after room for my book— in drawers, closets, underneath piles of clothes. Several times over, I searched the same places. I kept calling it my "Superman Book." I could not find it. Then suddenly, I had a big baby boy in my arms. He slept in my arms as I continued my search.

Eventually, I strolled to the front of the building with the child in my arms to look out of the window. I looked down just in time to see the big ship morph into a black tank. It was ready to launch. It would take off without me. Somehow, I knew it would. I did not seem to mind.

The tanker-boat detached from a big black metal bar and slid backwards down a steep rocky incline. The black tanker ran over a worker as it slipped off the cliff. Two other workers tried to rescue him, but they were unsuccessful. Suddenly, someone on the ground spotted me in the window with the child and tried to take a picture. I saw the camera's bright flash. Instinctively, I backed away from the window.

What was most clear to me about this dream was the spotted bride, representing the U.S. bride of Christ, was not ready for marriage to the Bridegroom. She was *not* "without spot or blemish." Big visible spots marked her face. The woman desperately wanted to be on the shabby vessel, and she made it. However, the ship she boarded was symbolic of a doomed ship like the Titanic.

By God's grace, there was no room for me on the boat. My Superman Book saved my life. Christ, the Living Word of God, is Superman. The Bible is His Book

There was a time in my life when I was on the lost boat, the sinking ship. In fact, I was so far from God, I had a suite of rooms on fated vessel. But the Lord changed all that. He redirected my path, which pulled me off the boat.

America, and everything she represents these days, is a sinking ship. The ship in my dream morphed into a "warship" (i.e., tank) at the end, suggesting the U.S. will be pulled into war. Chances are it will be a global one. America will not be victorious, because at the very end of the dream, the tank plummeted backwards off a steep, rocky cliff! *(Of Babylon, the Lord says: "And I will stretch out My hand against you, roll you down from the rocks" Jeremiah 51:25.)*

Jesus Christ, My Life Preserver

Having no place on the ship does not mean I will leave the country. I have no plans to leave the United States, although the Lord could send me away at any point. It does mean, however, that I have taken refuge in my Lord and Savior, Jesus Christ. He covers me. He keeps me. When I accepted His free gift of eternal life to cover my sin debt, He became, among other things, my Protector and Preserver.

As my Lord, Christ leads me in the way I should go. I follow Him, His Word, His commands. He commanded me to come out of the harlotries of the United States, and I did. When I did, I no longer had a place on the ill-fated craft.

As my Savior, Christ covered my sin with His own blood. Scripture makes it clear there is no forgiveness of sin without the shedding of blood (Hebrews 9:22). Christ shed His for me when He went to the cross, and through His blood sacrifice, I have eternal life. He invited me to come under His blood covering, and I accepted His invitation. The moment I did, He redeemed me to Himself, again pulling me off the lost liner.

I am *spiritually* covered by His blood. So, when the Death Angel comes at the time of judgment, and it will come as it did to the Egyptians and the children of Israel, it *must* pass over me as it passed over the Hebrews, because I am covered by the precious blood of the Lamb of God. Yes, I could lose my *physical* life when disaster strikes and the ship sinks, but I cannot lose my eternal soul.

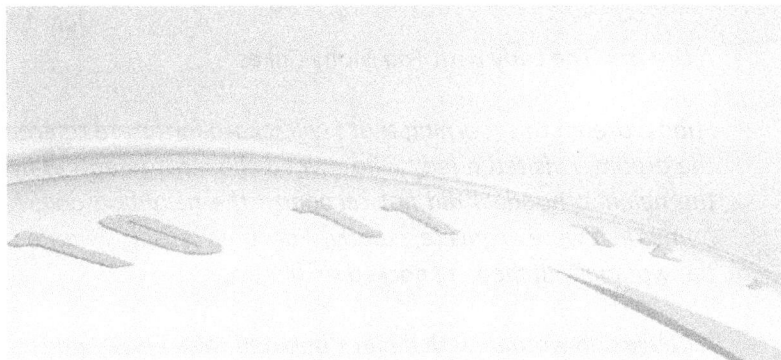

Chapter 9
The Spotted U.S. Bride

At the same time the Lord began the process of radically transforming my life, He revealed to me the spiritual state of the U.S. bride. She was like me. Neither of us was a lovely sight. Every dream He gave me about her was negative. Rather than infusing the culture around her with His light, she had become dark like the culture she was supposed to influence. She walked lockstep with the world.

In dreams, the Lord featured her asleep in La-Z-Boy recliners or on lavish high beds with lots of soft, puffy pillows, in well-appointed master suites with shiny hardwood floors. She was almost always overweight. Like the ancient Israelites, prosperity had lulled her into a deep sleep.

Three months after leaving the corporate business world, the Lord gave me a dream, in which He allowed me to glimpse the life of a typical American—a woman in bondage to the American Dream. My life, and that of His corporate bride, was not much different from hers. Like the typical American, we both had become entangled in the pursuit of mammon, and thus, were easy prey for the enemy.

July 12, 2007

A Dream: The Lady with Too Many Cakes

I had a dream this morning that I will record for future reference. In the dream, I visited a lady who owned the most beautiful house in the neighborhood. I did not recognize the neighborhood, but the homes in it were exquisite, stately. For some reason, I wanted to see the woman's kitchen. I knocked on her door.

A Caucasian woman with a black bob and thick black bangs opened the door. The hairstyle made her look like an ancient Egyptian. She was dressed in a black sweater and black pants. (Black is usually not a good sign in dreams.)

I explained to the woman she had the most beautiful house in the neighborhood. I asked to see her kitchen. I told her I was planning to renovate my kitchen and I would like to see hers. She allowed me in. The woman wore the most intense, joyless look on her face, an expression she carried throughout the entire dream. Not once did she smile.

As I followed her to the kitchen, I noticed she had rather wide hips. She explained her husband was on a business trip and he wanted her to fly out to join him. While she talked and I followed, I counted the cakes I saw in her house.

We walked from the foyer through the living room, through the dining room, and into the kitchen. Cakes were everywhere. Some were whole, some were partially eaten. Some appeared to be simply decorating the tables. I counted 13 cakes! I asked the woman about the cakes. "Why so many?" She never answered.

We walked into her kitchen. It was as plain as anything I had ever seen. It was also dimly lit and a bit dingy. I thought a few light bulbs had blown out. I exclaimed, "Oh, it's just a kitchen." I was not at all impressed. I thanked her and left.

As I exited her house, a hairy possum came up to me. It did not appear threatening. It seemed like it wanted to attack me, but I was not afraid. As it ran toward me, I said, "Oh, so you want to attack me? Come on because I'm tired of all this anyway!" I tried to swing at it with my brown purse—the one I carry these days in real life. The purse became entangled in my coat, so I half swung at it. The critter scurried off.

That is when I noticed three men hiding behind a tall bush. I spotted their feet first. I realized they were waiting to ambush me. I turned to go another way to avoid them. The dream ended with them following me.

The Egyptian-style woman—symbolic of someone in bondage—represented a typical American enmeshed in the American Dream. She was joyless, wasteful, and overweight. She lavished herself to excess, as evidenced by the 13 cakes. No matter how you slice it, no home needs 13 cakes! In Scripture, 13 is the number for depravity and rebellion, according to Ed F. Vallowe's *Biblical Mathematics— Keys to Scripture Numerics.*[1]

Surprisingly, the woman's kitchen was not at all impressive. It was dim, dingy, and quite unremarkable. In fact, her entire house was dim and unexceptional inside. It was beautiful on the outside only.

The house reflected the woman's life! (In dreams, a house is often symbolic of a person's life.) The woman's life looked great, even impressive on the outside, but on the inside, she was quite unremarkable. She was not at all pleasing to the Lord, hence, her all-black attire. The kitchen represented the heart of the house. It also

---

[1] Ed F. Vallowe, *Biblical Mathematics—Keys to Scripture Numerics.* The Olive Press, 1998, pp. 102-107.

symbolized the condition of the woman's heart—dark and in need of light.

The woman was not aware, and therefore, concerned about her dim house (life) or dark kitchen (heart). Her only concern was indulging herself—joining her husband on a business trip and baking (or buying) cakes. Thus, she was not fulfilled, which explains the gloomy expression she wore throughout the dream.

In dreams, a coat often represents a person's identity to the world. (For example, Joseph's coat of many colors identified him as Jacob's favorite son.) Thus, my purse becoming entangled in my coat was significant. My purse (i.e., reliance on money) was hindering me from discovering my true identity, who I was in Christ. In other words, my trust in money was hindering me from being all Christ called me to be and to do in this life. And because of this, I was ineffective in thwarting off enemy attacks (e.g., possum, three men). I was easy prey for them, just as the typical American is easy prey for Satan and his minions.

A month after giving me this dream; the Lord gave me another. In it, He showed me what He thought of His corporate bride. She was sinking under the weight of filth. He called her to be light and salt to the world around her. She was everything and anything but that.

August 10, 2007

A Dream: My Sister's Black, Sinking Car

I had two brief dreams the night before last. In the first dream, I saw my sister Arlene's car fall headfirst into a body of dark, murky water. I never actually saw my sister, just her car. Her car was black (not good). I saw the trunk of her car disappear into the gloomy water below as I peered over the ledge of a bridge. The scene changed.

Someone opened a window for me and counseled, "You can call to Him from here." I wanted to speak to my Father about my sister's car. I called to Him. I could see Him a short distance away. He was in a small semicircle of men, conversing. When I called, He looked my way.

"Have you seen my sister's car?" I asked Him. He told me not to worry about her car. "What I'm discussing over here will resolve all the family's woes," He said. I was not sure He understood my concern. I asked Him to come closer. The scene changed.

In the next scene, we sat right across from each other, face to face. I asked, "Do you know where her car is—my sister's car?" He said, "Yes." I asked Him where it was. He told me it was submerged in the dirty body of water. Now I was confident He understood my concern. The dream ended.

In my dreams, God always uses my sister Arlene to represent the U.S. Church. He did it again in this dream. My Father in the dream is my Heavenly Father. The men conversing with Him are angels. The black, sinking car represents the present destiny, direction of the U.S. Church. (The Lord frequently uses cars in my dreams to signal kingdom assignments, destinies, and the direction in which someone is headed.)

The dream plainly revealed how the U.S. bride is fulfilling her earthly mission from God's point of view. She isn't. Immersed in the dirty culture, she is quite ineffectual and unpleasing to Him. She has strayed far from Him and His precepts. Weak and powerless in ways she does not recognize, she is going down with the ship if she does not wake up and repent.

When the Lord releases His angels to execute judgment on the ungodly, she will be first in line if there is no change: "What I'm discussing over here will resolve all the family's woes," He warned. The U.S. Church is about to enter a time of great upheaval. She will be refined, perfected through suffering. The Lord is returning for a bride without spot or stain, whom He shall present to Himself. The refining fire awaits to burn off her every bond and blemish.

Chapter 10
Tyre and the U.S.—Sunken "Luxury Ships"

After revealing the sad spiritual state of the U.S. bride, the Lord showed me something in Scripture I never noticed before. The new insight greatly strengthened the bond between the sinking of the Titanic and the sinking of the United States. Through Ezekiel, the Lord brought a proclamation against Tyre, likening the ancient city's demise to that of a great luxury ship. He warned that He would sink the ship (Tyre) amid the seas! The moment I read it, I knew the sinking of Tyre was a shadow of a greater sinking to come—that of the U.S.

January 5, 2008

Tyre and the U.S.—Two Ill-Fated Ships

My time alone with the Lord this morning was long and insightful. He showed me much. I am utterly, totally, completely convinced that Ezekiel's lament and proclamations against Tyre and against its king in Chapters 26, 27, and 28 are layered passages that have application to the United States—just as God showed me 10 years ago.

What really gripped me this morning, however, was discovering that God compared Tyre to a luxury ship, a ship that He would sink. This was reminiscent of the Titanic!

In Ezekiel 27:3-11 and 25-36, the prophet compared Tyre to a beautifully-made luxury ship that traded with the nations of the world. God would sink that same ship (Tyre) in the midst of the seas. It had grown rich, proud, and arrogant. This was no coincidence; the sinking-ship metaphor was deliberate, a mere shadow of a greater sinking. The discovery linked Tyre's downfall with that of the U.S. What befell the early merchant nation was a type and shadow under the Old Covenant. Like all types and shadows, it concealed a hidden spiritual truth under the New Covenant of Christ: The U.S., a contemporary Tyre, would also go down like a lost luxury liner.

Verses 3-11

O Tyre, you have said, I am perfect in beauty. Your borders are in the midst of the seas. Your builders have perfected your beauty. They made all your planks of fir trees from Senir; they took a cedar from Lebanon to make you a mast. Of oaks from Bashan they made your oars; the company of Ashurites has inlaid your planks with ivory from the coasts of Cyprus. Fine embroidered linen from Egypt was what you spread for your sail; blue and purple from the coasts of Elishah was what covered you.

Inhabitants of Sidon and Arvad were your oarsmen; your wise men, O Tyre, were in you; they became your pilots. Elders of Gebal and its wise men were in you to caulk your seams; all the ships of the sea and their oarsmen were in you to market your merchandise.

Those from Persia, Lydia and Libya were in your army as men of war; they hung shield and helmet in you; they gave splendor to you. Men of Arvad with your army were on your walls around, and the men of Gammad were in your towers; they hung their shields on your walls all around. They made your beauty perfect.

Verses 3:25-36

The ships of Tarshish were carriers of your merchandise. You were filled and very glorious in the midst of the seas. Your oarsmen brought you into many waters. But the east wind broke you in the midst of the seas. Your riches, wares, and merchandise, your mariners and pilots, your caulkers and merchandisers, all your men of war who are in you, and the entire company which is in your midst will fall into the midst of the seas on the day of your ruin. The common-land will shake at the sound of the cry of your pilots.

All who handle the oar, the mariners; all the pilots of the sea will come down from their ships and stand on the shore. They will make their voices heard because of you; they will cry bitterly and cast dust on their heads; they will roll about in ashes; they will shave themselves bald because of you, gird themselves with sackcloth, and weep for you with bitterness of heart and bitter wailing. In their wailing for you they will take up a lamentation, and lament for you: "What city is like Tyre, destroyed in the midst of the sea?"

When your wares went out by sea, you satisfied many people; you enriched the kings of the earth with your many luxury goods and your merchandise. But you are broken by the seas in the depths of the waters; your merchandise and the entire company will fall in your midst. All the inhabitants of the isles will be astonished at you; their kings will be greatly afraid, and their countenance will be troubled. The merchants among the peoples will hiss at you; you will become a horror and be no more forever.

For years, God told me the U.S. would sink like the infamous luxury liner, the Titanic, but this was the first time He allowed me to see Tyre's end was like that of a sunken luxury ship. He was strengthening the metaphor between Tyre and the United States to expel all doubt that the two would suffer the same fate.

Chapter 11
King of Tyre's Tie to Satan

More than a year would pass before the Lord began to speak to me about the king of Tyre's unique connection to Satan. Sixteen months after God showed me in Scripture that He warned Tyre, through Ezekiel, that the nation would sink like a luxury ship in the seas, and He told me the same would happen to the United States, I made another unsettling discovery. Tyre's king foreshadowed the future Antichrist!

March 9, 2009
A Proclamation Against the King of Tyre (Ezekiel 28)

Never in the last 12 years have I understood so well the proclamation against the king of Tyre, prophesied in Ezekiel 28. Tyre's king was an Old Testament shadow of the future Antichrist! According to Scripture, Tyre's king was corrupted by sinister scheming in commerce and trade. And it is clear from Ezekiel 28:11-19, that Satan was the spirit behind the king.

Some could argue the description of the king in these passages matches the current President-elect, Barack Obama. For the first time, we have a president driving the nationalization of American businesses such as home mortgages, banking and investments, and the automobile industry. The President and his administration are deeply involved in commerce and trade in a way no other administration has been before, albeit their involvement is a result of a massive financial crisis birthed by past administrations.

In verses 11 through 16, God told Ezekiel to speak a lamentation against the king of Tyre. However, the prophet's discourse is clearly directed to Satan. Then, in verses 17-19, Ezekiel's proclamation of doom switches from Satan to the earthly king. The fact that one so easily melds into the other hints the two persons are interchangeable in God's eyes. They are one and the same. In fact, in verse 11 and 12, the Lord so much as calls the king of Tyre, Satan. In verse 11, Ezekiel directs his message against the king. Without a pause, in verse 12, he straightaway proceeds to describe Satan: *"Moreover the word of the Lord came to me, saying, 'Son of man, take up a lamentation for the king of Tyre, and say to him 'Thus say the Lord God: You were the seal of perfection, full of wisdom and beauty....'"*

The Prophet Ezekiel's Lamentation Against Satan (Ezekiel 28:11-16):

11 Moreover the word of the Lord came to me, saying, 12 'Son of man, take up a lamentation for the king of Tyre, and say to him "Thus say the Lord God: You were the seal of perfection, full of wisdom and perfect in beauty. 13 You were in Eden, the garden of God; every precious stone was your covering: the sardius, topaz, and diamond, beryl, onyx and jasper, sapphire, turquoise, and emerald with gold. The workmanship of your timbrels and pipes was prepared for you on the day you were created. 14 You were anointed cherub who covers; I established you; you were on the holy mountain of God; you walked back and forth in the midst of the fiery stones. 15 You were perfect in your ways from the day you were created, till iniquity was found in you. 16 By the abundance of your trading you became filled with violence within, and you sinned; therefore I cast you as a profane thing out of the mountain of God; and I destroyed you, O covering cherub, from the midst of the fiery stones."

The Prophet Ezekiel's Lamentation Against the King of Tyre or Antichrist (Ezekiel 28:17-19):

17 Your heart was lifted up because of your beauty; you corrupted your wisdom for the sake of your splendor; I cast you to the ground, I laid you before kings that they might gaze at you. 18 You defiled your sanctuaries by the multitude of your iniquities, by the iniquity of your trading; therefore I brought fire from your midst; it devoured you, and I turned you to ashes upon the earth in the sight of all who saw you. 19 All who knew you among the peoples are astonished at you; you have become a horror, and shall be no more forever.

I found this discovery beyond interesting. There was only one other place in all of Scripture in which a proclamation against a nation's king was a direct proclamation against Satan. God told the Prophet Isaiah to speak a lament against the king of Babylon, and when he did, he also spoke directly against Satan.

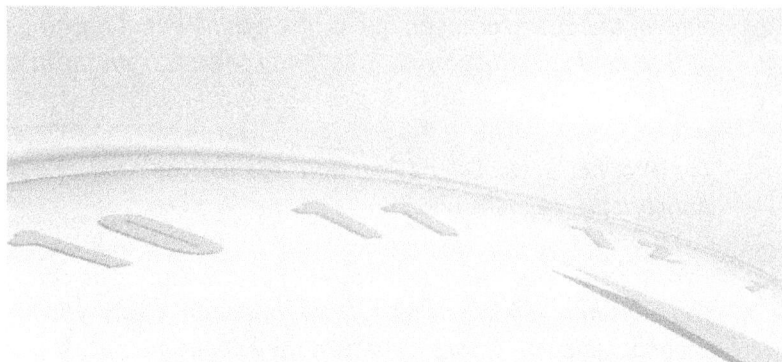

Chapter 12
Babylon's King Foreshadows the Antichrist!

The Prophet Isaiah did the exact same thing Ezekiel did—he prophesied against a human king and Satan simultaneously. In Isaiah 14, while speaking against the king of Babylon, Isaiah connected the king to Satan himself *and* to the future Antichrist. He linked Babylon's king to the Antichrist in a far more direct way than Ezekiel linked Tyre's king!

In Isaiah's description of the king of Babylon's fall, he first speaks of the earthly king's descent into hell after ruling the nations of the earth in wrath (vv. 3-11). The prophet then ties the king's downfall to Lucifer's fall from heaven (vv. 12-15). Afterward, Isaiah switches back to the Babylonian king. He is the one who makes the earth tremble; he shakes kingdoms. He is cast into hell for the making the earth a wilderness (vv. 16-20). That is exactly what the Antichrist will do.

The king of Babylon and Satan are interchangeable in the same way the king of Tyre and Satan are interchangeable. However, it is clearer in Isaiah's prophecy that the Babylonian king will do things that can only be attributed to the Antichrist. Name a ruler who has ruled all the nations of the earth in anger ... made the earth tremble ... shook nations ... destroyed all the cities of the earth ... and turned the planet into a wilderness. That is Antichrist's job description.

Further, verse 19 reveals the Babylonian king will be thrust through with a sword just as Satan was thrust through with by the Sword of Christ in April's dream! (See *April's Dream: The Rapture and a War in Heaven*, Chapter 5, p. 42.) The Babylonian king and Satan are interchangeable because they are the same person!

The Prophet Isaiah's Proclamation Against the King of Babylon or Antichrist (Isaiah 14:3-11):

3 It shall come to pass in the day the Lord gives you rest from your sorrow, and in your fear and hard bondage in which you were made to serve [speaking of Israel], 4 that you will take up a proverb against the king of Babylon, and say: 'How the oppressor has ceased, the golden city ceased! 5 The Lord has broken the staff of the wicked, the scepter of rulers; 6 he who struck the people in wrath with a continual stroke, he who ruled the nations in anger, is persecuted and no one hinders. 7 The whole earth is at rest and quiet; they break forth into singing. 8 Indeed, the cypress trees rejoice over you, and the cedars of Lebanon, saying "Since you were cut down, no woodsman has come up against us. 9 Hell from beneath is excited about you, to meet you at your coming; it stirs up the dead for you, and the chief ones of the earth; it has raised up from their thrones all the kings of the nations. 10 They all shall speak and say to you: 'Have you also become as weak as we? Have you become like us?' 11 Your pomp is brought down to Sheol, and the sound of your stringed instruments; the maggot is spread under you, and worms cover you.

The Prophet Isaiah's Proclamation Against Satan (Isaiah 14:12-15):

12 How you are fallen from heaven, O Lucifer, son of the morning! How you are cut down to the ground, you who weakened the nations! 13 For you have said in your heart: 'I will ascend into heaven, I will exalt my throne above the stars of God; I will also sit on the mount of the congregation on the farthest sides of the north; 14 I will ascend above the heights of the clouds, I will be like the Most High.' 15 Yet you shall be brought down to Sheol, to the lowest depths of the Pit.

The Prophet Isaiah's Proclamation Against King of Babylon or Antichrist (Isaiah 14:16-20):

16 Those who see you will gaze at you, and consider you saying: 'Is this the man who made the earth tremble, who shook kingdoms, 17 who made the world as a wilderness and destroyed its cities, who did not open the house of his prisoners?' 18 All the kings of the nations, all of them sleep in glory, everyone in his own house; 19 but you are cast out of your grave like an abominable branch, like the garment of those who are slain, thrust through with a sword, who go down to the stones of the pit, like a corpse trodden underfoot. 20 You will not be joined with them in burial, because you have destroyed your land and slain your people....

If the king of Tyre and the king of Babylon foreshadowed the Antichrist, it is only a short leap to the next question: Could the "king" or president of modern-day Tyre *and* Babylon the Great be the future Antichrist?

Chapter 13
Could a U.S. President be the Future Antichrist?

Given Ezekiel's treatment of Tyre's king and Isaiah's treatment of Babylon's king, one could argue the two kings—the king of Tyre and the king of Babylon—symbolized the satanic possession of a *single* leader of a *single* nation, a nation symbolic of *both* Tyre and Babylon. Since the United States is symbolic of both, is it conceivable the Antichrist is a past, present or a future president of the United States of America?

It is a fair question.

The Church teaches the Antichrist will rise from a cadre of European nations referred to as the Revived Roman Empire, described in Scripture as having seven heads and ten horns or crowns (Daniel 7:7-8, Revelation 13:1-2, and Revelation 17:9-14). It is this writer's view that we are witnessing the "Revived Roman Empire" in its embryonic state within the United Nations (UN). It is also this writer's opinion that the 44th president of the United States of America, Barack Hussein Obama, a figure of prominent stature within the UN, is the future Antichrist ("the little horn"). And, he will rise out of a ten nation-UN confederacy (i.e., 10 horns) during the last 3½ years of the age!

Perhaps, we are unable to see the forest for the trees.

The average American does not realize how many American thoughts, ideas, and philosophies have been influenced by the ancient Greek and Roman cultures. Much of Western Civilization is built upon Greek and Roman customs, conventions, and institutions. We can find evidence of Greco-Roman culture throughout every state in the United States in our architectural structures (e.g., colleges and university buildings, libraries, state capitals, and museums). Likewise, the architecture of many of our national institutions in Washington D.C., such as the Lincoln Memorial, Jefferson Memorial, Capitol Building, and White House, mirror ancient Greek and Roman edifices.

Greco-Roman influences on our country reach far beyond structural planning and design and into our democratic form of government, military strategies and tactics, language and literature, science and arts, mathematics, engineering, and law practices. Even our stadiums, where we watch spectator sports, are founded on ancient Rome's Colosseum, where thousands of Roman spectators from all walks of life, witnessed a variety of bloody spectacles—from gladiator sports to the mauling of Christians by wild animals. Before there was NASCAR, there was the Circus Maximus, where gladiators raced in horses and chariots.

We are more Roman than we know.

Scripture indicates the man of perdition may be a descendent of ancient Assyria, foreshadowed by the wicked Syrian ruler, Antiochus Epiphanes (Daniel 11:21-39). Related to this are several Scriptures that suggests God will have special dealings at the end of the age with Assyria's king and Assyria for their cruel and ruthless treatment of His people (Isaiah 10:12, 14:25, 30:27-33). Ancient Assyria spans the modern Islamic territories of Iraq, Turkey, Syria, and possibly parts of Iran.

Thus, Scripture hints that the devil will likely incarnate a modern-day Muslim. Surely, some will argue that Obama is not a Muslim, but a professing Christian. However, many who profess Christ have no real relationship with Him at all. Christ warned us that many on the Day of Judgment will call Him, "Lord!" They will try to remind Him of the things they did in His name, and He will say to them "Depart from Me, I never knew you" (Matthew 7:21-23).

If a person acts repeatedly against Scripture, which Obama has done, it may be assumed Christ's Spirit does not indwell that person. When a person's actions consistently produce fruit in direct contradiction to Scriptural precepts, it is safe to conclude Christ is not leading that person, despite what is professed. Actions reveal heart attitudes. Obama's real heart attitude will make him prey for a satanic incarnation.

Satan will entice the Antichrist to do his bidding. At the age's end, this man of sin will have the power to manipulate the world's commerce and trade system. Perhaps this will happen when the U.S. economy is severely weakened or collapses. Satan (disguised as Obama) will take deceitful and dishonest trade to menacing new heights. No one will be able to sell or buy without his mark (Revelation 13:17).

World Empires and Their Relationship to Israel

In a vision of the last days, the Prophet Daniel saw four beasts emerging from the sea. The first was an upright lion with eagles' wings. The second was a bear raised up on one side with three ribs between its teeth that devoured much flesh. The third was a leopard with four wings of a bird and four heads. But the fourth beast with huge iron teeth and 10 horns resembled no other animal on earth (Daniel 7:1-8).

Most scholars believe the four beasts represent the four dominant world empires of the past—Babylon, Medo-Persia, Greece, and Rome, respectively. It is this writer's considered opinion that we are viewing layered dominions *before* and *after* Christ's resurrection. His crucifixion and resurrection ushered in a new era in God's dealings with the world and its relationship to the apple of God's eye, Israel.

It is true that there are many Scripture passages that refer to ancient Babylon as both a lion and an eagle (Jeremiah 4:7, 49:19, 22, 50:17, 44, Lamentations 4:19 and Ezekiel 17:3). Likewise, in the Medo-Persian alliance, the Persians outpowered the Medes, thus aptly representing a lopsided bear. The agility and swiftness with which the Grecian Empire, under the leadership of Alexander the Great, conquered the Persians and Medes and other territories seem to point to a leopard with four wings. In addition, after his death, four generals (i.e., four heads) divided Alexander's expansive empire. Lastly, the Roman Empire, known for its cruelty and brutality, is described as being as invincible as iron in Nebuchadnezzar's dream, and in its revived state, having 10 toes of iron (mixed with clay). That is one layer of dominion.

Fast forward—past the crucifixion, burial, resurrection, and ascension of Jesus Christ—and the first three beasts in Daniel's vision can also represent modern nations of our own era: Britain (Lion), Russia (Bear) and Germany (Leopard). All three empires played a major role in the historic *resurrection* of Israel as a modern Jewish state under the New Covenant. Conversely, Babylon, Medo-Persia, Greece, and Rome were the key regimes that drove the historic *destruction* of ancient Israel (i.e., Southern kingdom of Judah) under the Old Covenant. The

Roman General, Titus, dismantled what remained of Israel (Judah) in 70 A.D.

In 1948, after nearly two thousand years, Israel was brought back to life as a Jewish State, thanks to the Lion, Bear, and Leopard. In his expose, "The Lion, the Bear, and the Leopard - Part 1," James Lloyd of *Christian Media Research*, does an excellent job in explaining why the three beasts represent Britain, Russia, and Germany.[2]

Britain (Lion) drafted the Balfour Declaration of 1917, which paved the way for the establishment of modern Israel as we know it today. That same year, the British army liberated Jerusalem from the Muslims. Throughout its history, an upright, crowned lion has been the official heraldry symbol of England's royal families. Some symbols even feature the British lion with eagles' wings. As America is most often associated with the great bald eagle, the removal of the eagles' wings in Daniel's vision could point to America's hard-won independence from the British Empire in 1776.

Russia (Bear) is well known for the persecution of Russian Jews. Russian "pogroms," fashioned to purge the empire of its native Russian Jewish population, fueled mass immigration to Israel. And no one will disagree that Joseph Stalin's Soviet Union devoured much flesh—an estimated 50 million people. The bear being raised up on one side could actually be a reference to Russia being the world's first leftist government that considered democracies, centrists, and those to the right, fascists.

Finally, Adolf Hitler and Nazi Germany (Leopard) swept across Western and Eastern Europe in a mad quest to annihilate Jews everywhere. Hitler's Third Reich named many of their armored tanks

---

[2] James Lloyd, "The Lion, the Bear, and the Leopard – Part 1", *Christian Media Research*. Christian Media Network. January 27, 2003. Web. May 5, 2012.

Panthers. (Note: Panthers and leopards in same family.) The two sets of eagles' wings (i.e., four wings) in Daniel's vision could represent the two key nations that allied with Nazi Germany—Italy and Japan. Furthermore, after Hitler's defeat, four military commanders (i.e., four heads) controlled Germany, under the Quadripartite Agreement. Freed by Allied Forces, Jews fled Europe to populate the newly formed state of Israel. Today, Jews are returning to Israel from all parts of the world.

Thus, Daniel's vision of the Lion, Bear, and Leopard looked toward the revival of Israel under the *New Covenant*. At the same time, the two regimes of Daniel's day (Babylon and Medo-Persia) and two to come (Greece and Rome) would successively contribute to Judah's demise as a kingdom under the *Old Covenant*. God will use the fourth beast to restore and reunite Israel's 12 tribes in the land promised Abraham, Isaac, and Jacob, under the headship of Christ, Messiah of the world!

The Fourth Beast

The fourth beast in Daniel's vision was described as "dreadful and terrible and exceedingly strong," and it was different from the first three. The text hints that the fourth beast is a modern offspring of the ancient Rome Empire, which much of today's Western Civilization is. Perhaps, the fourth beast resembles no known animal because it is a conglomeration of many nations, a multinational assemblage of evil. The Antichrist will come from this fourth beast. He is referred to as the "little horn" in the passage below:

> After this I saw in the night visions, and behold, a fourth beast, dreadful and terrible, exceedingly strong. It had huge iron teeth; it was devouring, breaking in pieces, and trampling the residue with its feet. It was different from all the beasts that were before it, and it had ten horns. I was considering the horns, and there was another horn, a little one, coming up among them before whom

three of the first horns were plucked out by the roots. And there, in this horn, were eyes like the eyes of a man, and a mouth speaking pompous words (Daniel 7:7-8).

Presently, the United States, Russia, and England have three of the five permanent seats on the United Nation's Security Council. France and China hold the other two permanent seats. (Germany left the Security Council in December 2012 to become a regular UN member.) Only the five nations holding permanent seats have veto power on the Council. Ten other nations hold non-permanent seats on the Council. This 15-member body is responsible for the maintenance of international peace and security. It presides over all global nuclear discussions. It is possible this configuration could be reduced to just 10 nations in the future, under one head—the Antichrist. It appears the snare has been set. It will be turnkey tyranny when Satan snaps the trap shut.

The Lord also gave the Apostle John a similar vision of the fourth beast. It, too, suggests the Antichrist will rise to power from a council of nations. Again, Germany (Leopard), Russia (Bear) and Britain (Lion) are identified as major players in this multinational assembly. Satan (i.e., dragon) is the true power behind this international ruling body, and he will be the authority behind the Antichrist's throne:

Then I stood on the sand of the sea. And I saw a beast rising up out of the sea, having seven heads and ten horns and on his horns ten crowns, and on his heads a blasphemous name. Now the beast which I saw was like a leopard, his feet were like the feet of a bear, and his mouth like the mouth of a lion. The dragon gave him his power, his throne, and great authority (Revelation 13:1-2).

Revelation 17 also speaks of the fourth beast, but in riddle form. Out of the seventh empire (i.e., a multinational conglomeration), will come an eighth—the Antichrist's empire.

Here is the mind which has wisdom: The seven heads are seven mountains on which the woman sits. There are also seven kings. Five have fallen, one is, and the other has not yet come. And when he comes, he must continue a short time. The beast that was, and is not is himself also the eighth, and is of the seven, and is going to perdition. The ten horns which you saw are ten kings, who have received no kingdom as yet, but they receive authority for one hour as kings with the beast. These are of one mind, and they will give their power and authority to the beast. (Revelation 17:9-13).

The seven kings represent seven dominant world empires. Five have passed ("fallen")—ancient Egypt, Assyria, Babylon, Medo-Persia and Greece. During John's time, Rome still existed ("one is"). And the "international council of nations" or UN did not yet exist ("has not yet come"). It is from this global legislative body the Antichrist will arise. It is from this base of power and leadership Satan will birth the eighth (and final) world empire. It will last only 3½ years or 42 months.

How might it happen that Obama can go from being President of the United States to King ("Pharaoh") of the entire world? I am not sure. But I am confident it will involve a hell-inspired assassination, in which Satan himself will cunningly usurp Obama's identity and earth's throne. Once Satan is sitting in Obama's seat of power and wielding supernatural wonders within the UN, he can mastermind all kinds of deceptions to conquer and intimidate heads of nations to do his will. From a UN power base, the man of perdition can mislead and ultimately subjugate the world's masses.

This is not as far-fetched as you might think.

On April 10, 2013, the Lord gave me a dream, in which Barack Hussein Obama suffered a mortal head wound! In the dream, he suddenly disappeared, vanished and a sinister man-beast stood in his place. The beast resembled an animal *and* a man. And it was clear he was a beast of war, and he would shed much blood.

April 10, 2013

A Dream: Obama's Head Wound and the Beast

It is now 5:54 in the morning. I just woke up from a dream. In the dream, I found myself looking up and out of an old warehouse window. My surroundings suggested I was out in the middle of nowhere. A lot of open land surrounded the warehouse. I saw a few small structures in the distance.

Suddenly, I saw up close the backs of government men in dark blue windbreakers. They were standing near the warehouse, facing outward away from the warehouse. Their backs were to me. The words ATF came to my spirit, although I never saw the words on the back of their jackets. I saw one agent smoking a cigarette. Then something happened.

I looked away from the cigarette-smoking agent toward a long dirt trail, a short distance away. I saw Obama. He was dressed in a grey suit and white shirt. He had been shot in the head! Two men in dark blue windbreakers were on either side of him, holding him up. A white bandage had been wrapped around his head. It was bloodied from a wound.

Suddenly, a furry growling THING appeared where Obama had been! Obama was gone. The THING was covered completely in brown fur, like a bear, but it walked upright like a man and it growled things to people and itself. It had a long assault weapon in its hand. The thing was a beast of war.

At first, its back was to me. Then, it slowly turned around. I saw its face. It had the face of an animal with dark black circles for eyes, yet it appeared to be a man.

It looked directly at me through the little window in the warehouse, which seemed impossible since the window was so small and high up. It knew I was in the warehouse, peering at it! An overwhelming terror struck my heart. "It's here! It's here!" I kept whispering to myself.

In Revelation 13, one of the heads of the fourth beast suffers a fatal head wound! But it is miraculously healed:

And I saw one of his heads as if it had been mortally wounded, and his deadly wound was healed. And all the world marveled and followed the beast. So they worshipped the dragon who gave authority to the beast; and they worshipped the beast saying, "Who is like the beast? Who is able to make war with him?" (Revelation 13:3-4).

My friend, Gina Hockaday, who has an extraordinary prophetic gift, sent me an email a week before my dream that read: "God just told me a drastic change is coming to the White House!" I suspect my dream revealed what that change will be. An event is, indeed, coming that will change the White House, and thus, the country and ultimately the world.

It appears Barack Obama, sometime during his political career, will suffer a head wound. Alcohol, Tobacco and Firearm (ATF) agents will be around or involved when he is shot. The wound will prove fatal. However, because Obama disappeared and, in his place, was the beast—the Antichrist—Satan will incarnate his body. He will make it appear as if the wound was not fatal. From that point on, the United States and the world will be dealing with Satan himself. The assault rifle in the hand of the beast indicates the Antichrist will promote conflict and war. Woe to the earth!

"Ides of March" and "Spring Forth"

Three months *before* the assassination dream, on January 13, 2013, the Lord gave me a dream in which I tried to explain to my ministry partner, Suzanne Eustache, what Ides of March meant. I told her a pattern had been set. What happened before will happen again. Something will repeat.

The Ides of March is a specific day on the Gregorian calendar, March 15. The date is widely associated with the assassination of the Roman Emperor, Julius Caesar, by the Roman Senate. The senate feared the king would destroy their republic with his tyranny. It led to civil war.

In my dream, the words "spring forth" were somehow connected to Ides of March. Not only did I hear the words, spring forth, and try to explain to Suzanne what they meant, I saw them handwritten on a poster board. I told her spring forth had something to do with a vast push, rush, or movement of people.

Upon awaking, I immediately associated Ides of March with a coming political crisis in the U.S. At the time, I postulated a betrayal of some sort would lead to Obama's assassination, but I was not sure. I further theorized the assassination would lead to a national crisis. The crisis would spring forth and trigger a mass uprising, maybe even civil war.

After seeing Obama suffer a head wound in a dream, I became convinced the Ides of March expression pointed to Obama being betrayed and assassinated, possibly on a future March 15. His death would not produce the result the conspirators intended. Instead it will hatch a plot that will lead to the massacre of many since Satan, invisibly pulling all the strings, is waiting in the wings to completely take over the planet!

The Counterfeit Bride (Church)

It is also this writer's position that sometime during the Great Tribulation, the Church of Rome, deeply corrupted by this time, may act as the spokesperson for the counterfeit church. She will rise to prominence after the true bride (Church) is raptured—in support of, and in partnership with, the Antichrist. The Antichrist and the False Prophet will orchestrate The Great Apostasy, a worldwide false religion (described more fully in Chapter 20). The resurgence of the Roman Church in this manner will most certainly contribute to concept of a "revived" Rome in all its ancient glory, although the revival will be short lived.

Since Rome sits on seven hills, the reference to "the seven heads are seven mountains on which the woman sits" in Revelation 17:9 may be a direct reference to Church of Rome at the age's end. (The seven heads and seven mountains are distinguished from the seven kings mentioned in verse 10.) It is through this counterfeit church the Antichrist and Rome will propagate a worldwide system of false religion to deceive the masses. Many believers of Christ will be martyred during their reign.

So he carried me away in the Spirit into the wilderness. And I saw a woman sitting on a scarlet beast which was full of names of blasphemy, having seven heads and ten horns. The woman was arrayed in purple and scarlet, and adorned with gold and precious stones and pearls, having in her hand a golden cup full of abominations and filthiness of her fornications. And on her forehead a name was written: Mystery, Babylon the Great, The Mother of Harlots and of the Abominations of the Earth. I saw the woman, drunk with the blood of the saints and with the blood of the martyrs of Jesus. And when I saw her, I marveled with great amazement (Revelation 17:3-6).

During his brief time in power, the Antichrist will eventually destroy both Babylon the Great (U.S.) and the closely aligned counterfeit church. However, God will be behind their destruction:

And the ten horns which you saw on the beast, these will hate the harlot, make her desolate and naked, eat her flesh and burn her with fire. For God has put it into their hearts to fulfill His purpose, to be of one mind, and to give their kingdom to the beast, until the words of God are fulfilled. And the woman whom you saw is that great city which reigns over the kings of the earth (Revelation 17:16-18).

The short-lived amalgamation of 10 nations, headed by the Antichrist, will viciously rule the world, making it inhospitable. Nuclear missiles will undoubtedly be the nations' weapon of choice. This 10-nation league will be hell bent on Israel's destruction, as were five of the past six world empires (Egypt, Assyria, Babylon, Greece, and Rome). But its destruction by the Lamb of God will pave the way for a fully revived and united Israel! *These will make war with the Lamb, and the Lamb will overcome them, for He is Lord of lords and King of kings, and those who are with Him are called, chosen and faithful (Revelation 17:14).*

Satan's chief goal is to be worshipped as God by earth's inhabitants. He will use the U.S., the United Nations, and all his wonders to assume earth's throne. He will attempt to destroy Israel, believers in Christ, and anyone who stands in his way, making the earth desolate in the process.

As head of the world, the Antichrist will also seek to devour the male child in Revelation 12. As the woman in Revelation 12, who is expected to give birth to a male child at the end of the age, I can expect to be stalked by the beast until the Lord removes me and the child from the earth.

The Dawning of a New Day

As discussed more fully in Book One, *The Spotted Bride*, the male child in Revelation 12 is really two different male children at two different points in history. One is Christ (Revelation 5a). The other is His son, Joshua. Joshua is symbolic of Christ's body *and* the reunification of the 12 tribes of Israel at the final dismantling of a Gentile-ruled world, under Satan's sway. Thus, Joshua represents the dawn of a New Day, in which Christ, who purchased earth's title deed at the cross, will rule the planet.

Until I give birth, and the child and I are caught up to God's throne, the Lord will protect me. In fact, God gave me a short dream the same morning He gave me the assassination dream, in which it was written in the clouds of the sky: "She lived to tell it." God will keep me alive to warn others.   After the child and I are snatched up, the Great Tribulation, spanning 3½ years or 42 months—the last half of Daniel's 70th Week—will commence (Revelation 12:6).

The same morning, I dreamt about Ides of March and spring forth, I researched the phrase, spring forth. The Scripture verse, Isaiah 43:19, was one of the first posts to appear: *"Behold, I will do a new thing, now it will spring forth. Will you not see it? I am making a way in the desert and streams in the wasteland."*

The verse is associated with God suddenly delivering His people from Babylonian captivity just as millennia earlier He delivered their forefathers from Egyptian captivity by parting the Red Sea. The passage also points to a greater fulfillment of this promise through Jesus Christ, who will deliver the whole world from the wilderness Satan and man's sin create. It points to a day when Gentiles will be converted to Christ and Israel (Judah and Ephraim) will be united into one house, under Messiah, and recalled to her land.

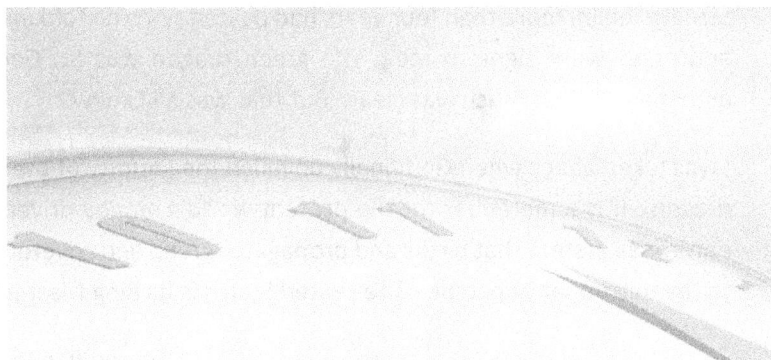

Chapter 14
The Green Dragon-U.S. Connection

On September 11, 2009, The Ephraim Project, our ministry to help the "poorest among us," began serving Orlando's homeless at St. George Orthodox Church. The moment Father John, the priest, opened St. George's doors to us, I finally understood the reason my old address on Royal St. George Drive was a sign to me. Shortly after Suzanne and I moved there in July 2005, God told me the address was to serve as a sign to me. For the life of me, I could not understand why.

I came to discover that Saint George is one of the most venerated saints among Eastern Orthodox Christians. He is also revered in the Catholic, Anglican, East Syrian, and Ethiopian Churches. He is immortalized in literature, on murals and frescoes, in paintings and other works of art, slaying a green dragon. At St. George Orthodox Church in Orlando, he is recognized as a defender and protector of the poor, infirm, and impoverished. After this discovery, I knew our ministry to Orlando's poorest residents would blossom under the martyr's name.

A week after we began serving at St. George, the Lord finally revealed the significance of my former landlord's address—Green Dragon

Street! Again, more than four years had passed since he told me *both* addresses were signs to me. The green dragon was St. George's archenemy. That much was clear. But that was all I knew.

I was taken aback when God finally unveiled the identity of the green dragon. It is a metaphor for the present world's money-driven, free enterprise system that births and propagates greed and covetousness to the detriment of people. The United States is its Ring Master!

September 16, 2009

Slaying the "Green Dragon"

This morning when I least expected it, God shed light on the whole "St. George-slaying-the-green-dragon" business. Suzanne and I resided on Royal St. George Drive in Orlando for more than four years, leasing a home from a landlord, who moved his family residence to Green Dragon Street. At first, I was blind to the significance of the street names. But God opened my eyes when I visited the Coptic churches in Ethiopia.

On my return flight to the States, it occurred to me that Jesus Christ, His mother, Mary, and St. George were painted on the walls of all the Coptic churches in Ethiopia. Further, St. George was always on a white horse, slaying a green dragon. A princess was usually in the background. She was the king's daughter. St. George saved her from the dragon.

At that point, I realized that I had been given a dot to connect to the two addresses. Sitting on the plane, I kept asking myself, "What are the chances that of the tens of thousands of addresses in Orlando, my landlord would move to Green Dragon Street after leasing his home to me on St. George? He and his wife were as blind to the significance of the street names as I was. Clearly, God had orchestrated both of our relocations.

The two addresses were to serve as signs to me, the Lord long ago counseled. Eventually, I figured out the St. George part after we began serving the poor at St. George. But who or what was the green dragon? God finally gave me a clue in the wee hours of the morning.

I rose a little after 4 a.m. to read my Bible. I picked up where I last left off in the Book of Ezekiel, Chapter 31, which dealt with Egypt's downfall. God likened the ancient nation to a tall tree that needed to be cut down because of its pride and arrogance. Instantly, I knew while the passage spoke about ancient Egypt, it also foreshadowed a "modern-day Egypt" that would be cut down by the Lord. The passage pertained to the fall of the U.S. and ultimately the world!

Felling a Tree

As I read the passage, I was suddenly reminded of an object lesson the Lord gave me in Memphis, Tennessee. It was a nasty lesson. He gave it to me to help me understand that one day soon He would cut down a "tree" of His own.

In Memphis, a city patterned after ancient Memphis, Egypt, I was forced to cut down a tall tree on my property. Hundreds of foul birds came to nest every evening in that tree. It created the worse stench one can imagine. There were other trees surrounding this one, but the birds never touched them. They congregated in this one tree.

People walking down the street would cross over to the other side to avoid coming near my property. Every few days I had to clean their foul droppings from my walkway and wood fence. If I missed too many days, the stench would overwhelm everyone who came near my house.

I did everything to keep from cutting down that tree—from using powerful jet sprays of water on the birds, dousing the tree with heavy chemicals, to placing big fake owls (their natural predators) in its branches. Nothing worked. The birds returned every evening to foul the tree and my owls. I decided I had no choice but to get rid of it.

I called Dr. Ugly. (Yes, the literal trade name of the business was Dr. Ugly!) A few days later, Dr. Ugly's handsome son showed up at my door, while his crew waited outside. Dr. Ugly did not come himself. He sent his son. (I am not making this up!)

"You're Dr. Ugly?" I asked in amazement.

"No," he gently smiled. "I'm actually Dr. Ugly's son. Show me the tree."

In a matter of mere minutes, the tree was gone, stump and all. I could not even tell the tree had ever existed after Dr. Ugly's son was done! The birds never returned. God told me He would do the same to the U.S. through His own "Dr. Ugly's Son to come!"

In Ezekiel 32:2, God compared Egypt to a sea monster or sea serpent (Rahab). Some commentators say the mystery creature is a sea monster, a sea serpent, a sea dragon, a crocodile, or an ancient dinosaur. However, Ezekiel says of Pharaoh, king of Egypt: *"… you are like a monster in the seas, bursting forth in your rivers, troubling the waters with your feet, and fouling their rivers."*

In God's eyes, Egypt's king was the Leviathan that fouled many waters. That verse led me to several others that I never considered before. I discovered Rahab was a monster in ancient pagan mythology. God used the sea monster to symbolize Egypt throughout the Old Testament (Ezekiel 29:3, Psalm 87:4, 89:10, Isaiah 30:7).

After that, I discovered a prophecy by Isaiah that referred to that same sea monster—Egypt—that God cut to pieces. In the latter days, just like He did with Egypt in ancient times, He will cut off all oppressors to free His people:

Awake, awake, put on strength O arm of the Lord! Awake as in the ancient days, in the generations of old, are You not the arm that cut Rahab apart, and wounded the serpent? Are You not the

One who dried up the sea, the waters of the great deep; that made the depths of the sea a road for the redeemed to cross over? So the ransomed of the Lord shall return, and come to Zion singing with everlasting joy on their heads; they shall obtain joy and gladness; sorrow and sighing shall flee away (Isaiah 51:9-11).

Suddenly, I realized whenever God spoke of Rahab, He was not speaking of a literal or mythical sea dragon, monster, or crocodile. In the same way He used the "felling of the tree" to symbolize the cutting down of Egypt, He was using the "slaying of a sea serpent" to symbolize the destruction of a Satan-inspired nation and a world system it helped birth!

The green dragon is a metaphor for a world system that thrives on the seas and in ships. It pollutes the waters of the world and defiles nations. Ultimately, it enslaves the peoples of the world in a never-ending quest for mammon to the exclusion of their Creator.

In the system's wanton, ruthless pursuit of money and profits, there is little or no room for the poor, alien, or outcast. The weak and powerless are pushed out or aside. They are either a reproach to, or forgotten by, the privileged. That is the reason God's servant, St. George, seeks to defend and protect them.

A nation taken captive by this greedy, covetous spirit is demonically inspired and controlled by that serpent of old, Satan. And while this sea creature of a system can overwhelm man, it is no match for God. Scripture indicates God will slay the green dragon, cut it down in due season. (Interestingly, green is the color of U.S. currency.)

When the sea monster is slain, our world system of commerce and trade, as we know it, will become extinct. Perhaps, after that is when the Antichrist will step in and establish a brief 3½-year commerce and trade system to regulate the world's masses. He will rule the peoples of the world by manipulating and controlling the global economic system. People everywhere must take his mark to buy or sell.

Ten months after breaking the green dragon code for me, the Lord reminded me of it again. God always establishes a matter with at least two witnesses (Deuteronomy 17:6, 19:15, John 8:17). The reminder made the destruction of the green dragon system, a certainty.

July 9, 2010

Slaying a Green Dragon—Revisited

This morning while reading Ezekiel 26 and 27, I saw clearer than ever the United States, a modern version of Tyre, as the arrogant sea monster or dragon that sits in the midst of the seas and pollutes the waters and other nations through corrupt trade and commerce. Chapter 26 revealed how Tyre will be destroyed, while Chapter 27 delineated in detail the many nations that traded with Tyre and what they traded.

Tyre became excessively wealthy, but the great wealth corrupted her and her many trading partners. In God's eyes, Tyre's system of commerce tainted the waters via its ships that carried their abundant cargo for trading. Metaphorically, the seas were sullied by the world's foul and corrupt trading processes. Thus, the dirty sea monster had to go.

Suddenly, I am also reminded of the millions of Africans who lost their lives en route to the Americas during the Transatlantic Slave Trade. These men and women were tossed into the sea like rubbish, refuse when they died or rebelled. Those who survive the journey were taken to work the sugar cane and cotton fields of their new masters. In God's eyes, this trading and trafficking of people literally polluted the waters in ways the profit-seeking slavers could not see.

Reading large swaths of passages in Ezekiel 26 and 27, I could easily substitute the U.S. for Tyre. The only conclusion I could come to was the world's commerce and trade system—led by the U.S.—is a modern-day sea monster that contaminates the waters of the earth through unethical goods (and people) trafficking. God will put a stop to it. Ezekiel proclaimed God would cause many nations to come up against Tyre *"as the sea causes it waves to come up, and they shall destroy the walls of Tyre and break down her towers"* (Ezekiel 26:4). Tyre, likened to a luxury ship, would go under, and so would the U.S.

Satan is the spirit behind the world's warped commerce system—a system in which mammon rules. When people are forced to chase money in order to survive, perverse things happen. The poor, weak, and powerless are not seen as people to help, but objects to exploit. For example, China is well known for incarcerating her citizens—many for their faith in Christ—and forcing them to work to produce goods to export to the U.S. and the rest of the world. The slave labor results in competitive prices that produce greater corporate profits. As consumers of these goods, we turn our heads and pretend it is not happening.

In our corrupt commerce system, politicians are bought and sold by the rich and powerful. These policymakers are used by Wall Street Titans to shape and influence government policy at all levels—federal, state, and local—to support and benefit big money interests. This often happens at the expense of the impoverished or disenfranchised. This is in direct conflict with Scripture's repeated admonitions to protect the weak, poor, and powerless.

In this dark "bull" system, if the poor are not exploited for greater profits, they are simply ignored, rejected, or forgotten. Clearly, in this present age of darkness, Mammon is King, an idol many worship—just like Baal ("the Bull") was worshipped by Israel in Elijah's day. God will demolish all Baal worship, once and for all, in the dreaded Day of the Lord.

The Green Dragon of the United States of America (and the world) will be cut down by God's Son, Jesus Christ (a.k.a. Dr. Ugly's Son). He will have His day. He will collapse the world's monetary system. When the U.S. monetary system falters, the rest of the world will be thrown into utter chaos, a bedlam the planet has never seen.

Chapter 15
A Lesson from Pompeii

On December 31, 2011, after viewing a Discovery Channel documentary on the sudden destruction of the ancient city of Pompeii, *Pompeii: Back from the Dead*, the Spirit of the Lord began to speak to me about how the destruction of the U.S. will parallel Pompeii's. The nation's ultimate destruction will be the result of a series of disasters, not just one. And despite God's repeated warnings, many will be caught unawares. It will be business as usual right until the last moment.

Three months before I saw the documentary, the Lord gave me a vision of three rings of fire lying on a large body of dark water. For the longest time, I did not know what the vision represented. I inquired of the Lord many times. But on the day—just hours before I watched the Pompeii documentary—the Lord revealed to me there is an area in the Pacific Ocean called the "ring of fire." It is known for its high seismic activity. I do not believe in coincidences. There is a connection between this ring of fire and America's sinking.

I am convinced the Pompeii documentary and my three-rings-of-fire vision are linked to the dozen or more tsunami-flood dreams the Lord has given me through the years. In three of the dreams, a massive tsunami hits crowds of people unexpectedly, out of nowhere. In one dream, the sky is clear and blue, and then there is a thunderous sound, followed by a massive wall of ocean water coming toward me and others. It barrels through the streets, consuming everything in its path. I, and the two people with me, start running. We only take two steps before we are overtaken.

In two other dreams, I am being carried away by flood waters and appear to be drowning. Both times I am trapped in a sinking car. In another dream, I am alone, and I witness all types of debris floating past me as I stand on a semi-elevated porch. Things are in the water that ought not to be—bridges, cars, refrigerators, furniture, you name it.

In still other dreams, I am with other people, surrounded by a sea of water. Water is on all sides. Nearly everything is submerged as far as the eye can see—land, houses, everything. We appear to be survivors of an epic flood.

Typically, a tsunami is released by seismic activity (e.g., earthquake) underneath the ocean bed. This shifting in the earth's crust underneath the ocean dislocates tons of water. The water is carried in waves at great speeds toward land. By the time it reaches the coastal areas, massive tons of water have been displaced, and like an enormous voluminous, liquid freight train, the torrent can plow through a coastal area, washing away anything and everything in its path—cars, buses, trains, homes, buildings, even skyscrapers. The water can travel several miles inland, flooding whole neighborhoods.

Several years ago, I saw a vision of the map of the United States. Large swatches of the nation's coastal regions—from the Northeastern seaboard down through the southeastern and southwestern U.S., up

Book Three: The Late Great United States

to the West coast—were wiped away, submerged under water. Florida was completely gone.

In my dreams, I have also seen the destruction left by a huge earthquake or series of earthquakes on land. Devastation is widespread. The landscape is completely upended. It looks as if a bomb exploded. It appears many states are impacted.

In one dream, I witness several semi-tractor trailer trucks and cars unable to stay on the highway. Then I realize why. The drivers are not drunk, which is my initial thought. The earth is swaying, moving. The drivers cannot control their cars or rigs. Crashes follow and pile up.

In other dreams, I see what appear to be nuclear blasts on American soil. In one, I witness the surrounding landscape of a whole neighborhood melt away. Something catastrophic happens, and the homes quickly disintegrate and melt away. Other nations watch the destruction and the aftermath of it, on television.

In the same way, many people may not realize the residents of Pompeii were killed, not by a single catastrophe, but by a series of disasters, suddenly without warning.

January 1, 2012

Take a Lesson from Pompeii

Last night I saw a documentary on the destruction of the ancient city of Pompeii, Rome. While I watched, I could easily superimpose any modern American city over Pompeii and see the same immoral lifestyle themes and patterns. Its destruction serves as a warning to us modern Romans today.

Now archeologists believe the volcanic eruption that spewed massive layers of ash over the city, burying its lava-encased residents for centuries was just one in a series of catastrophic occurrences that week. They believe it all began with a large earthquake, in the already earthquake-prone city. They speculate half of the residents fled the city after the earthquake in 79 A.D.

However, those who remained experience utter destruction not more than a week later when Mt. Vesuvius erupted. The cities of Pompeii and Herculaneum lie at the foot of this mountain. Both cities were completely destroyed.

Following are some insights I gleaned from the documentary as the Spirit spoke to me:

1. *The destruction came at the high point of Roman society. The Roman seaport of Pompeii had become the playground for the rich, powerful, and famous. Many Romans had holiday villas there. The city was rift with sexual immorality and sexual perversion—same sex, any age, orgies—as revealed by the painted frescoes. On August 24, 79 A.D., the city was suddenly destroyed without warning. Thousands of unsuspecting people, ranging from super rich Romans, to merchants, to craftsmen, to slaves, were destroyed "suddenly without remedy" (Proverbs 29:1, 6:15).*

2. *The Lord, in His mercy, gave people a small window of opportunity to escape with their lives, to leave everything behind. It was the same offer He gave Lot and his family in the destruction of Sodom and Gomorrah. Some Pompeiians seized the opportunity and fled. Others, like Lot's wife, could not leave their possessions. There are signs in the ruins that residents who left their homes and businesses were looted after the first event, so some people may have stayed behind to protect their interests, thinking the worse was over. But the earthquake was only the beginning.*

3. *The greed and covetousness of some people would be their undoing. Within a week, those who stayed behind witnessed a volcanic eruption that spewed black debris up to 20 feet into the air. This, alone, would have stricken deep fear in the*

hearts of most residents since they did not know the mountain was an active volcano. The two cities that rested at the foot of the mountain began to be pelted first with little rocks the size of a Ping-Pong ball. But as the larger rocks dislodged and spewed out from inside the mountain, the people began to be hit with massive pieces of sediment. It was like a hailstorm of rocks and boulders.

4. *Some archeologists believe the volcanic activity cut off the water supply to the city. Having no water only compounded the troubles of the people in ways we cannot imagine. But this, too, would soon make no difference.*

5. *The rain of pumice and black ash came next. The ash fell at about four feet per hour for six hours. It eventually buried the entire city, so no one would even know a city once existed there. The ash alone would have turned broad daylight into night, preventing people from seeing even a few feet ahead.*

6. *After the ash came the hot lava, traveling at the speed of a jet airliner! The hot lava encased men, women, children, animals, pottery, coinage, fruit, meals—everything where it stood or lay. In what seemed like an instant, everything and everyone was encrusted. There was no chance of escape. Thousands were crushed during a mad rush out of the city. The riotous stampede created a human gridlock at the city gate, trapping residents. All were consumed by hot lava.*

7. *Last of all came the noxious fumes that slowly suffocated the remaining residents, who had managed to escape all the other calamities. Their bodies were found hiding in tunnels and cellars.*

There are several instances in the Bible in which the Lord warned a people to repent. In almost every case, only a remnant heard and responded. A few fled the city as they were warned and escaped destruction. It was business as usual for the rest.

Then one day, like any other day, disaster struck without warning. There was no remedy for the disobedient. There was no escape. Every soul the Lord had tapped for ruin on the day of doom was destroyed.

If the sword did not get them, famine did. If famine did not get them, disease did. If they escaped disease, wild animals were sent as the Lord's instrument of judgment. In one instance, the Lord tracked those targeted for destruction all the way into the land of Egypt and destroyed them there (Jeremiah 44). For a short while, these Judean residents thought they had managed to save themselves from the siege of Jerusalem. They escaped without heeding God's warnings to stay put. They did not know God was coming for them. It is a terrible thing to fall into the hands of an angry God.

While watching the Pompeii documentary, what gripped me most was I knew the fate of the people. I knew they would be completely destroyed. Their destinies were sealed. But in the reenactment of the events of that week and final day, I could see the people did not know they would be utterly consumed. They had no idea of what was coming.

We see some snatching up and hiding their precious jewels and treasures, perhaps thinking they will need these to rebuild their homes or lives. Others refused to leave their homes or businesses. They had too much at stake. Thieves would have a field day. Everything they worked so hard to build would be lost. Looters, at least for an instant, perhaps thought they could suddenly have the things their hearts longed for. Maybe the treasure, albeit ill gotten, could be used to transform their lives, even bring them out of poverty or slavery.

The one thing all these people had in common was that they put too much stock in their present lives and none in their eternal. They put all their longings, desires, expectations, aspirations, ambitions, and cares into the things of this present world and forgot about their eternal souls. Everything the human eye can see will one day be destroyed, but a soul lives for all eternity.

There is nothing, absolutely nothing, more tragic than a human soul condemned to hell for eternity. Repent, my dear brother or sister, while there is still time. Cry out to God to save your soul. He will.

Beloved, the Lord is calling His people out of Babylon the Great. We are to come out of her, or we will share in her plagues. We will be destroyed with her. In just one day, on a day like any other, Babylon the Great will be consumed by fire. The Lord is warning us to let go of the stuff and flee for our lives … our very souls!

On the same day I recorded the journal entry about Pompeii's destruction, I wrote this about my "three-rings-of-fire" vision and its connection to a sudden destruction of the United States:

January 1, 2012

The Three Rings of Fire—A U.S. Connection

On September 24, 2011, I saw a vision of three rings of fire—two small, identical rings inside a larger ring. All three lay on a large, dark body of water. It appeared to be night. Today, I learned there is an area of high seismic and volcanic activity called the "ring of fire"—stretching from New Zealand in the South Pacific, up through Japan, across to Alaska and down the west coasts of North and South America. (Note: For the past year, Japan has been rift with seismic activity, and even today experienced a 6.8 magnitude earthquake.)

I sense the ring of fire will play no small role in America's destruction. Perhaps, seismic activity in this area will ultimately trigger an earthquake on the West Coast of United States. The West Coast quake will be the catalyst for at least two other earthquakes that will split the U.S. apart, dividing the nation the length of the 2,320-mile long Mississippi River. The Mississippi River—the fourth longest in the world—rises from Northern Minnesota and runs southward through Wisconsin, Iowa, Illinois, Missouri, Kentucky, Tennessee, Arkansas, Mississippi, and Louisiana to the Gulf of Mexico.

As in the case of Pompeii, the earthquakes will be only the beginning. Based on other things the Lord has revealed to me, I suspect the country will experience flooding of epic proportions as tsunamis consume the coastal areas, and the Mississippi, Missouri and Ohio Rivers flood inland states. It all may have the effect of the country sinking like a ship in water, just like the Titanic.

A final gleaning from the documentary on Pompeii was that God had His instruments of destruction ready and in place, just waiting for the set and appointed time. The people of Pompeii had no idea the festive Roman city, which rested at the base of Mount Vesuvius, would one day be consumed by a volcanic blast. They did not know the mountain had the potential to erupt and wipe out their city's existence and that of Herculaneum.

God's instruments of doom may sit dormant as unassuming parts of the landscape for centuries, even for thousands of years, with no one realizing the deadly destruction they will one day wrought. In the days of Noah, no one had ever seen rain. However, a liquid canopy covered the earth from the time of creation, so when it came time to judge the people, the canopy burst, pouring rain over the earth for 40 days and 40 nights. Not only that, the foundations of earth below ruptured, spewing floodwaters upward. Only eight people survived the epic rain and flood waters. Prior to that Day of Judgment, the residents of earth were not aware of God's inbuilt instruments of destruction surrounding them.

Orlando, Florida is called by some The City of Lakes because lakes dot the landscape. Most residents do not know that the city is built on an aqueduct. So, although located in Central Florida, and not near the Atlantic Coast, Orlando could be flooded in an instant should it experience an earthquake. A city, state, or region may look safe, but in the Day of the Lord, there is only one safe place: in the will of God, because only He can save an eternal soul.

Chapter 16
Revisiting the Titanic-U.S. Sinking

In March 2012, the Lord began to expand upon the Titanic-U.S. metaphor with renewed intensity. Surprisingly, He used our family's home and our faithfulness to Him and His Word as an example of the kind of people who will escape His judgment (or the fateful sinking). With the 100th anniversary of Titanic's demise fast approaching, He also chose to reveal things about the ship's sinking that I never knew before. Then He linked these things to the downfall of the U.S.

March 18, 2012

Signs of Coming Chaos and Judgment

I am seeing the number 11 everywhere! It does not matter which direction I turn my head or what I am doing, God always puts the number 11 in my face! In Scripture, 11 is the number for chaos and divine judgment.[3] Also, for at least the last two weeks, I have seen many things pertaining to the sinking of the Titanic. Titanic—The Experience is a local exhibit; it must be on every bus billboard in town.

---

[3]Ed F. Vallowe, *Biblical Mathematics—Keys to Scripture Numerics.* The Olive Press, 1998, pp. 94-97.

Last week, I saw a documentary about the Titanic as well as a modern reenactment of the sinking. New photographs of the sunken ship and new theories on why and how it sunk are flooding the public media. The blockbuster movie, The Titanic, *is about to be re-released in 3-D.*

Perhaps, this is happening because the 100th anniversary of the ship's sinking is only a month away, April 15, 2012. Or something bigger, more ominous is looming and God is moving around the chess pieces to forewarn us.

Just this afternoon at church, an Orthodox priest donated a box of 26 hardback books to The Ephraim Project. Each of the 26 books contained anywhere from 5 to 6 stories—that's roughly 130 to 156 stories. At random, I picked one book from the large pile. Without examining the cover, I flipped it open. My eyes fell on a story entitled, The Night Lives On. *It was a sequel to* A Night to Remember *by Walter Lord. The story was about the sinking of the Titanic! (What are the odds?)*

March 21, 2012

"Twenty Minutes to Twelve"

My most recent dream about the rapture came on the heels of a conversation I had with the Lord at about 2:40 this morning. I woke up with something that had been on my mind for hours, even while I slept. I wanted to discuss it with Him.

Just after I fell asleep around 10 o'clock last night, I awoke to God's voice speaking to my spirit. I distinctly heard: "twenty minutes to twelve." Immediately, without doing any calculations, I said out loud to my empty bedroom: "That's 11:40 p.m." After drawing that conclusion, I quickly extracted four others from the phrase:

1. *That is the exact time the Titanic hit the iceberg.*
2. *Forty is the number for trials and testing.*
3. *Eleven is the number for chaos and divine judgment.*

4. The Church of Philadelphia ("The Faithful Church") will be safe when God sinks the United States (Rev. 3:7-13).

In our early-morning conversation, the Lord told me "twenty minutes to twelve" pointed to a certain fact: The wicked were on a collision course with Him. His repeated warnings had gone unheeded. One day soon, when everyone least expects it, as it was with those on the seemingly "unsinkable" Titanic, disaster will strike. For the wicked, it will be a disaster without remedy. Their souls will be lost forever. This will be the fate of the faithless. The Lord promised the fate of the faithful will be different. He revealed my childhood home—unbeknown to my family and me—symbolized the Faithful Church of Philadelphia!

Our House on Philadelphia

I lived with my family at 4011 W. Philadelphia in Detroit, Michigan from birth to age 16. For most of my life, I did not know that the numbers 40 and 11 in our address were acutely significant. In Scripture, 40 is the number for trials and testing, 11 is the number for chaos and divine judgment.[4] Our street name was also significant. Philadelphia means "brotherly love."

After age 16, we moved across town to another home, where my family lived until I went to college. My parents sold the second house and purchased a third one that my younger brother owns today. As a family, we had many sweet and bitter experiences in all three homes. But the Lord chose to make the house on Philadelphia the setting of so many of my dreams and visions. Finally, He revealed the reason. For many years, as the number 40 in our house address indicated, we were a family on trial, in a test. In fact, frequently, tossed and

---

[4] Ed F. Vallowe, *Biblical Mathematics—Keys to Scripture Numerics*. The Olive Press, 1998, pp. 94-97 and 173-176.

afflicted—one trouble after another—my mother often moaned, "It's like we're a family on trial!" We were particularly tested in extending brotherly love to others as Christ commanded in His Word. Often, He asked us to give to others when we had so very little for ourselves. My parents and siblings passed this test with flying colors. Growing up, our house was like Grand Central Station. My parents helped many individuals and families get on their feet. And each of us followed in our parents' footsteps as we journeyed through life. We cared for many people who were not our own. Our family was a microcosm of "The Faithful Church" in Revelation 3:7-13. God commended this body of believers for its faithfulness to Him and His Word.

In Revelation 2 and 3, when Christ visited the seven churches, only the churches of Philadelphia and Smyrna, "The Persecuted Church", received passing grades. Christ told the Philadelphian body that she would be kept from the *"hour of trial that will come upon the whole world to test those who dwell on earth" (Revelation 3:10).* The hour that will come upon the whole world to test its residents is the Great Tribulation—a horrific time of chaos and divine judgment:

I know your works. See, I have set before you an open door, and no one can shut it; for you have a little strength, have kept My word, and have not denied My name. Indeed, I will make those of the synagogue of Satan, who say they are Jews and are not, but lie—indeed I will make them come and worship before your feet, and to know that I have loved you. Because you have kept My command to persevere, I also will keep you from the hour of trial which shall come upon the whole world, to test those who dwell on the earth (Revelation 3:7-10).

The Lord gives the Philadelphian church four reasons why she will not suffer His wrath in the Judgment:

1. Her strength is small. She is not strong, powerful, and mighty.

2. She keeps His Word. The Faithful Church chooses to live by God's Word in a crooked, upside-down world that hates God, His precepts, and teachings.

3. She never denies the Lord's name. Bitterly afflicted and persecuted by the world, but she clings to Him and His promises.

4. She never gives up. She keeps the Lord's commandment to persevere, against all odds.

Those faithful to God and His Word will be kept and preserved on His Ark of Safety when He pours His wrath on the nations. All others will go down with the ship!

The Titanic and God's Ark of Safety

The day before God put Lord's book, *A Night to Remember*, in my hands, He spoke to me about two metaphoric ships that will mark the end of the age. One is Christ, a type of Noah's Ark. He is a place of safety and refuge, especially when flood waters sink the U.S. The other is the United States, a type of Titanic. It is unsafe. The Lord indicated I represented a type of Noah. Just as Noah had been called to warn and prepare his generation for God's coming judgment, I had been called to warn and prepare mine.

The Lord stressed those who cling to the Him and His Word during this Dreadful Day will find safe refuge in His Ark, as did Noah and his family 4,200 years ago, when the flood waters covered the earth. It was a time of worldwide judgment. All others, who chose *not* to cling to Him and His Word during this second time of worldwide judgment (by fire, not water) will be lost. It will be certain doom for those seeking passage on the Leviathan.

Following is a comparison of the two ships:

Christ/A Type of Noah's Ark	U.S./A Type of Titanic
God designed Ark; Noah and three sons built it ("Let God do it.")	Men designed Titanic; 15,000 men built it ("Let us do it.")
Passengers: God-focused; dependent on God	Passengers: Self-focused; independent of God
Owner's/God's Interest: Brotherly Love	Owner's/JP Morgan's interest: Profits (Mammon)
Godly; invisible and spiritually based	Worldly; visible (physical) and senses based
Destination: Promised Land/Heaven	Destination: New York City, symbolic of the "broad way" (i.e., wide road to death and destruction)
Completely safe, unsinkable	Appears safe, but easily sinkable
Members diverse and inclusive	Members diverse, but exclusive (Titanic passengers sharply segregated into three distinct classes)
Operated by poor, despised, considered foolish of the world	Operated by rich, powerful, mighty of the world
Attitude: Humble, modest; man is errant and must depend on God	Attitude: Proud, materialistic, Edwardian—world of abundance, extravagance, indulgence, amusement; man is capable of achieving anything and, thus, does not need God

Christ/A Type of Noah's Ark	U.S./A Type of Titanic
Plain, modest; poor to tattered	Every imaginable luxury
Few resources	Abundant resources
Passengers prepared for time of disaster	Passengers unprepared for time of disaster
Discerned God's 11th hour warnings	Did not discern Captain Lord's warning that came as late as 11 p.m., 40 minutes before iceberg collision
Stopped, heeded signs	"Shut up! Shut up! I'm busy!" (Titanic's First Officer to Captain Lord of the California, a nearby ship that warned of icebergs ahead. California could have saved all Titanic passengers.)
Slowed down and listened	Did not listen ("Full speed ahead")
Faced—head on—issues, obstacles, challenges of having life in Christ	Skirted around issue with fatal results. (Experts say a head-on collision with iceberg could have saved the Titanic; a maneuver around iceberg ripped open the ship.)
Many left comfortable lives to do as God commanded	Many passengers did not want to leave the comfort of the ship for small lifeboats until it was too late

Christ/A Type of Noah's Ark	U.S./A Type of Titanic
Tested and proven; escaped judgment	Hit iceberg at 11:40 p.m. Did not pass test, judged
Families remained intact (e.g., Noah's entire family saved)	Families separated and torn apart forever
Final state of passengers: safe, kept, protected, humbled, and grateful for life; filled with hope for the future	Final state of passengers: alone, fear, terror, despair, regrets; all is lost—loved ones, possessions, future, eternal souls

Fascinatingly, Christ, our Lord and Savior of Mercy chose Lord Mersey (Pronounced "mercy") to preside over the British panel investigating the sinking of the Titanic. Accusations and finger pointing was the order of the day. But instead of penalties being imposed, under the leadership of Lord Mersey, the sinking gave rise to new shipping regulations.

About three weeks after the Lord gave me the two-ship comparison, the movie *Titanic* was re-released. Although I saw the film before, God wanted me to see it again. He arranged a special viewing for me.

April 13, 2012

Titanic, The Re-Released Movie

Today, I had an unexpected date, arranged by God. By 1:30 p.m., all I had planned to do for the day was done. For someone who works 12 to 14 hours a day, this was quite unusual for me. Everyone I called had no time to chat. To kill time, I drove to the post office to mail a letter and then to the bank to deposit a check. I looked at my day planner to see what I could move up to do from another day. Nothing. Then it hit me. God had freed up my schedule for a reason.

Yesterday, I told the Lord I felt as though He wanted me to see the re-released Titanic, but I had no time. I would not dare go after work since the film is three hours long, and I would probably be asleep after the first hour. Besides, I would not get home until nearly midnight and my days start early. I left it at that.

Suddenly, I realized I was close to the movie theatre. Remembering our conversation from the day before, I wandered over to the theatre to check the times. Sure enough, there was one that would start in less than an hour.

I grabbed a slice of pizza next door, checked my voicemail one last time to be sure I did not have a crisis to handle. No messages. I purchased my ticket. The agent gave me a pair of 3D glasses and a special ticket holder that resembled a boarding pass to the Titanic.

I walked into the theatre with my two-dollar bag of popcorn—a special that day—to find my seat. Not another soul joined me. The theatre was all mine! Confident now that God had arranged the date, I picked a middle seat in the middle of the theatre, and I pulled out my notepad and pen. I resolved to mine for golden nuggets during the viewing.

Following are some of the gems I found after seeing the film again:

1. Things were not as they seemed. Losers were really winners. The two men who lost their tickets on the Titanic to Jack and his friend in a poker game were really winners. Likewise, many who now appear to be losers in the U.S. are really winners, and many who appear to be winners are really losers.

2. The ship appeared unsinkable, yet it took only 2 hours and 20 minutes to sink. Likewise, the U.S. appears invincible. Yet, it will be destroyed in one hour. Western States will sink into the Pacific Ocean. Flood waters from the Great Lakes, Mississippi, Missouri, and Ohio rivers will overflow the Central

U.S. all the way to the Gulf of Mexico, and the Atlantic Ocean will cover the Eastern shorelines as well as Florida. The U.S. will sink just like the Titanic sunk into the Atlantic.

3. The Titanic was called "A Ship of Dreams" just as the U.S. is known for "The American Dream." Many immigrate to the U.S. to pursue their dreams of finding wealth and prosperity. The Titanic was filled with such people and others who had already attained great affluence.

4. The night the Titanic sunk, the skies were clear and the water calm. Disaster did not seem imminent. And so it shall be the day (or night) God judges America.

5. The sinking of the Titanic was a "sudden disaster without remedy"—no one could answer the ship's distress calls. And so shall it be with the sinking of the United States.

6. As we approach the end, there will be panic, civil unrest, and rioting in America just as panic and disorder ruled on the Titanic in the end.

7. As we approach the end, the rule bound will try to control the masses, to enforce rules, not realizing the dark (spiritual) rulers of this world and their Satan-inspired system have been overthrown.

8. As we approach the end, people will try to make business deals to save their lives. The deals will not work. The deals will not spare their souls.

9. Those who survive the unraveling of the nation will survive because they "hear what the Spirit is saying." Spiritual discernment will prove far more profitable than the reliance on the five senses. (Rose to Jack: "It doesn't make sense. That's why I trust it.")

10. Those who are lost will be like those on the Titanic—laughing, partying, drinking, and even playing music until the very end.

11. Masses will die in the sinking of the U.S. More than half of the Titanic's passengers perished.

James Cameron's *Titanic* was first released in 1997, which was the year my strange journey began with the Lord. Interestingly, 1997 was the Hebrew Year 5758, which means "Season of Noah." Also of note, the day God pulled me out of Corporate America—the day I "jumped ship"—was April 10, 2007. The Titanic's maiden voyage began April 10, 1812.

It was significant that on the 100th anniversary of the sinking, the Lord would have me revisit the film. The body of Christ has entered a special season. A time of unprecedented upheaval is just around the corner. During this period, the unimaginable will overtake the United States of America. She will fall and sink in the midst of the seas.

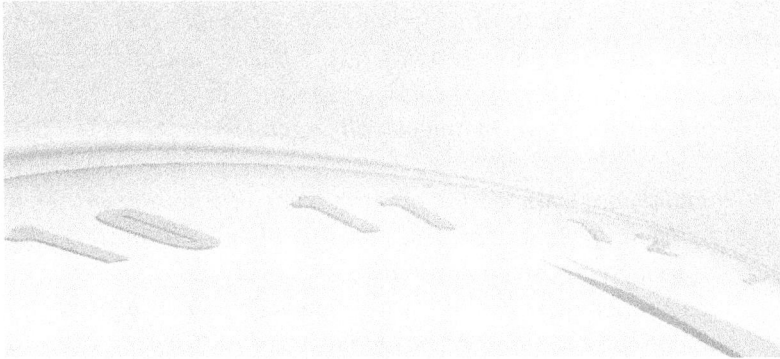

Chapter 17
Tyre and Titan: Two Foreshadows, Two Witnesses

After I returned from viewing the re-released *Titanic,* that same day, I discovered the book, *Futility* by Morgan Robertson. The novella spoke of the sinking of a luxury liner named Titan in the North Atlantic. The ill-fated vessel was sunk by an iceberg. *Futility,* authored by a man named Morgan, seemed to foretell the sinking of the Titanic, owned by J.P. Morgan, 14 years before it happened!

How could that be? I knew there was more to it than met the eye, so I inquired of the Lord. He blew my mind with what He revealed. The ship Titan in *Futility* foreshadowed the sinking of the Titanic, just as the sinking of Tyre foreshadowed the sinking of the United States. Together, they served at the two witnesses He requires to settle a matter (Deuteronomy 19:15, 2 Corinthians 13:1b).

April 13, 2012

Futility

Futility means that which is "useless" ... "vain"... "poured out." The word reminds me of Solomon's often quoted phrase in Ecclesiastes: "All is vanity." Life lived on earth apart from the Creator and Author of Life is "chasing the wind." It is all vanity, futility!

It does not matter if a person builds an entire civilization with his bare hands. If Christ is not in it, the builder and the civilization are ultimately doomed. It can look spectacular to the world. But it is only for a season. In time, it will crumble.

Futility, not surprising, is also the name of a novella written in 1898 by Morgan Robertson. The novel is about a disgraced U.S. naval officer, who became an alcoholic, but found redemption and restoration after finding Christ. However, there is a part in the story about the sinking of an ocean liner named Titan. Written 14 years before the sinking of the Titanic, the Titan's sinking bears an eerie resemblance to the sinking of the Titanic. It foretells the Titanic's fate.

Following are the striking parallels between the two ships:

	Titan	*Titanic*
Length	*800 feet long*	*882 feet long*
Passenger capacity	*3,000*	*3,000*
No. of Passengers	*2,500*	*2,200*
Touted	*World's largest, unsinkable*	*World's largest, unsinkable*
How It Sunk	*Hit an iceberg*	*Hit an iceberg*
Speed at Time of Collision	*25 knots*	*22.5 knots*
Date of Sinking	*April*	*April 14, 1812*
Place of Sinking	*North Atlantic/400 miles from Newfoundland*	*North Atlantic/400 miles from Newfoundland*
Side of Ship Hit	*Starboard side*	*Starboard side*
Lifeboat Capacity	*Less than half for all passengers*	*Less than half for all passengers*
Death Toll	*More than half died*	*More than half died*

Unless one is completely deluded, and many people are, the similarities between these two ships cannot be dismissed as coincidence. There is no such thing as coincidence, chance, or happenstance in the Kingdom of God. Rather what we see in the pattern is a righteous, merciful God, once again, trying to get the attention of a blinded, busy people, lost in their everyday earthly burdens, cares, and pleasures. The Lord is about to shake land and sea. He is trying to get those who can hear His Spirit at this hour to WAKE UP! TAKE REFUGE IN CHRIST! AND COME OUT OF BABYLON!

The Lord is speaking to the United State of America: "YOU are the arrogant, proud, luxurious 'Titanic' that is about to be sunk!" Remember the Titanic, called "Queen of the Sea," was built and launched in Belfast, Ireland, but it was a U.S. enterprise, financed by J.P. Morgan. Likewise, the disgraced naval officer, John Rowland, who found redemption and restoration in Christ in the novella, *Futility*, was a U.S. naval officer. Yes, the God of the Universe is speaking to YOU, America!

According to Scripture, God requires at least two witnesses before a matter is settled. For example, He gave Pharaoh two dreams to warn him that, that which seemed impossible was surely going to happen: the Breadbasket of the World, Egypt, would experience a devastating, seven-year famine. The nation's wealth would be wiped out. The two dreams were a warning to Pharaoh to get ready, be prepared. Pharaoh heeded the warning. Seven years later, the famine hit. It was just as God had revealed it to him in the dreams and just as Joseph had interpreted the dreams by God's grace.

In connection to Pharaoh's two dreams, the Lord gave Joseph two dreams when he was 17 years old. He told Joseph that his brothers, in fact, his entire family would one day bow down before him. How could that ever be? Under what circumstances could that ever happen? At age 30, Joseph rose from a prison felon to become governor of Egypt. He was second only to Pharaoh. Moreover, he controlled the storehouses of Egypt during that time of great famine.

As God would have it, Joseph's brothers had to travel to Egypt to secure grain for the family during the famine. Sure enough, they bowed on their knees before Joseph, who controlled the storehouses. Eventually, Joseph's brothers and their families, his father Jacob, and Jacob's remaining two wives—70 in all—traveled to Egypt to escape the devastating famine that had gripped the world. There, Joseph cared for them. Again, God's Word came to pass.

In the same way God forewarned Pharaoh and Joseph, He has provided for our consideration as U.S. citizens two metaphoric witnesses of a coming national disaster—Tyre and the Titanic. We would do well to heed what they are saying to us.

As discussed earlier, in the ancient world—millennia before the United States—there was a nation strikingly similar to the U.S., the city-state of Tyre. All the nations of the ancient world traded with Tyre, and she became extraordinarily great. As Tyre, a merchant nation situated on the seas, grew in unprecedented wealth and prosperity, she became proud and corrupted and filled with sexual immorality. She worshipped the work of her hands and not God.

The Lord likened Tyre to a luxury ship that He would eventually sink, if she did not change her ways. She did not and He did. As Ezekiel prophesied, she ended up like the "top of a rock" and a place for the "spreading of nets" (Ezekiel 26:4, 5). Interestingly, Babylon the Great (a.k.a. the U.S.)—Tyre's modern twin—will share a similar fate. Jeremiah prophesied she will end as a "burnt mountain" in the midst of the seas (Jeremiah 51:25, 42).

Tyre is to the United States as the Titan is to the Titanic. The Titan foreshadowed the sinking of the Titanic. Tyre foreshadowed the sinking of the U.S. The United States has been taken captive by the same demonic spirit that took captive Tyre. Thus, the U.S. will share Tyre's fate. The true Church must come out of her (spiritually) before God's judgment sinks the nation.

God is warning all who can hear, while there is still time: "Come out of Babylon the Great!" He is warning us to take cover in the shed blood of the Lord and Savior, Jesus Christ. He is our Ark of Safety. Only He can save us eternally. Jesus Christ is God's Plan A. There is no Plan B. God is about to shake heaven, land, and sea. Only those covered by His blood will be saved. The Death Angel cannot touch their souls. It will pass over them. But those not found in Christ will perish forever.

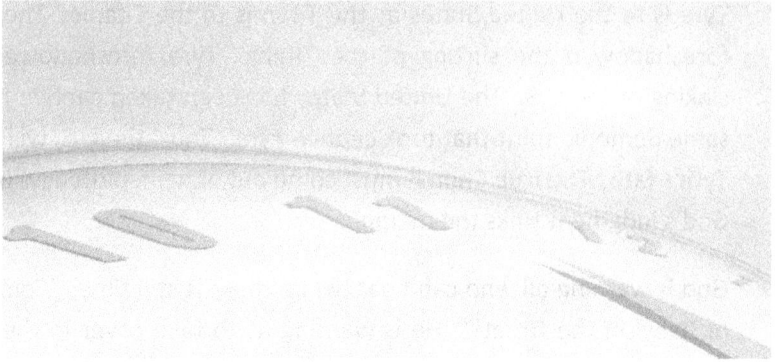

Chapter 18
Judging America's Idols

What is an Idol?

God has always had an issue with idols. He makes no bones about it. He hates them. They compete with Him for our attention and affection. They cannot save us. Only He alone can. They distract us from what is important and can send us straight to hell for all eternity. Only God, and God alone, is worthy of our undying devotion and worship. We are to worship the Creator and not created things.

Throughout Scripture, God caused peoples' idols, their gods, to fail them. When God decides to judge a nation, He often begins by toppling their idols—things, objects, systems, institutions, even people, they rely on and put their faith in, instead of Him.

Idols are not just little fat, bald figurines. They are those things people allow to consume their time, attention, energy, and resources to the exclusion of God. Look at your checkbook and calendar. How and on what are you spending God's money? How are you using the time He gave you on earth? When we pour ourselves into anything other than

God, we are, in effect, exchanging Someone extraordinarily valuable for something quite worthless. God will not stand for it.

Egypt's Idols Toppled

When God judged ancient Egypt for the enslavement of His people, He began to dismantle the infrastructure and institutions the people relied on. For example, the Nile River was the lifeblood of Egypt, its major water source. People needed water for a multitude of reasons—drinking, cooking, bathing, household chores, watering livestock, and more. The first plague God sent upon Egypt turned the Nile River into blood. Even water that had been pulled from the river before Moses struck it with his staff, turned to blood.

Surely, the plague killed all fish in the Nile and adjoining tributaries and ponds. It must have produced an unimaginable stench throughout the nation. Picture the effect of having no fresh water on Egypt's economy! Still, Pharaoh refused to listen.

As Pharaoh's heart continued to harden, God upped the ante. He ruined Egypt's land (grain fields and farms) with frogs, lice, and flies. He eventually destroyed Egypt's livestock—cattle, horses, donkeys, camels, oxen, and sheep—with pestilence. The Egyptians depended on their water, land, and livestock for their everyday livelihood just as much as they relied on their pagan deities. These were the critical foundations of life—the "gods" that sustained them. Who was this "I AM" Moses spoke of?

Hailstones sent from heaven obliterated every herb and plant in the field and shattered every tree. Whatever the frogs, lice, flies, hail, and pestilence did not destroy, the locust swarms did! All that made Egypt great—the breadbasket of the known world—was reduced to nothing. Everything they (and past generations) had achieved and poured their lives into, the Lord smote. A civilization that took hundreds of years to build was wiped out within a short time span.

God wanted Pharaoh to set His people free so they could worship Him in Spirit and in Truth. God's people were too busy making bricks for Pharaoh to devote any time to God. They had been enslaved 430 years! They were the backbone of Egypt's economy! How could Pharaoh let them go? What would happen to Egypt? Every time Pharaoh refused God's command to let His people go, God hewed away another sector of Egypt's economy. Eventually, He destroyed the nation's entire infrastructure.

Finally, God moved to slay the firstborn in every household whose doorpost was not covered with the blood of an unblemished lamb. This foreshadowed the protective blood of Christ, the Lamb of God. The children of Israel knew what to do because Moses gave them instructions. But the Egyptians were clueless. So, when the Death Angel passed over Egypt, a mass slaughter occurred. All firstborns were killed in a single night—from firstborn babies to firstborn adults to any firstborn animals that were left. All were no more.

Even after this great personal and national loss, Pharaoh would not let God's people be. After releasing them, he went after them. He wanted the Hebrews back. Egypt's economy depended upon them. This defiance costs Pharaoh his army! In an attempt to bring back the Israelites, Pharaoh's army—equipped with the finest bred horses and chariots of the day—drowned in the Red Sea. In a contest of might, it is insane to tangle with the Almighty!

Toppling America's Economy

If God is to be worshipped for who He is—God Almighty, Maker of heaven and earth—then He must remove all competitors. He will destroy *any* and *all* things that keep His people from worshipping Him as God.

God has already begun to dismantle the economy of the United States. There is absolutely no question. The Lord is toppling our nation's economy since we have made mammon our god. In the U.S., Cash is King, not Christ. We worship the Almighty Dollar. God has no choice but to destroy the dollar. The American dollar continues to lose value against other currencies of the world. One day, in the not too distant future, it will be completely replaced.

In September 2008, when our economy faltered, causing other economies to tumble across the globe, many nations lost confidence in the dollar. Even many Americans lost confidence in the dollar, exchanging it for gold and other precious metals.

Since September 2008, there are many countries, including many developing ones that no longer trade in American currency. They do not trust it. They prefer to deal in their own currency or other world currencies, like the Euro, Pound, or Yen.

This author suspects a clandestine movement is already underfoot by China and other nations of the world to replace the dollar as the world's standard of currency. These nations, most likely under the future Antichrist's direction, will unexpectedly replace the dollar. Then, America would have become her creditors' booty. (See Habakkuk 2:7).

Toppling America's Housing Industry

In the U.S., we worship our homes. God began to disassemble the U.S housing market several years ago. He allowed the mortgage industry and the greedy Wall Street Titans to blow it apart. We have only just seen the tip of the iceberg here.

Most Americans spend large portions of their lives trying to acquire and maintain a home. Many Christians do this to the exclusion of God and those things He has called us to do as people of Light in a dark, crooked, upside-down, hurting world. We will go to work to pay our mortgage or rent before we will go to a sanctuary to praise and worship God. We invest significant percentages of our time, energy, and resources into the purchasing, maintaining, and beautifying our homes, while the rest of the world starves, spiritually and physically. God must demolish this idol in our lives.

Today, more than 10 million Americans have lost their homes to foreclosure. In every city, houses sit empty with few buyers willing to invest in them. More houses will swell their ranks in the coming months and years.

Toppling America's Businesses

American business—from major corporations and national retail chains to midsize companies to small mom and pop shops—are going belly up all over the nation. Drive down any American thoroughfare in any city or town and witness the empty buildings—storefronts to skyscrapers. "For Lease" signs are everywhere. The list of companies that have gone bankrupt or are teetering on the brink of insolvency since 9/11 is astounding.

The pace of failed companies accelerated after the September 2008 economic meltdown. The disappearance of businesses from local communities spell a loss of city and state tax revenue, leading to the insolvency of many city and state municipalities. Today, Detroit sits completely bankrupt. According to a recent survey by *Newsmax Media*, at least 20 other American cities face the same fate.

The business sector is where America's great sin found its birthing chamber. As our free enterprise system grew strong and powerful, we began to worship the work of our hands and forgot God. We believe we built our nation into the global superpower it is today. It was our own beauty, brains, and brawn that made us great. We became like gods in our own eyes. But there is only one God, and He will not share His glory with anyone.

Toppling America's Jobs

Our jobs and careers, which consume most of our waking hours, will go the way of our houses. As businesses continue to fail, we will lose more jobs and careers. They will simply disappear from the economic landscape.

In our modern society, our jobs and careers represent our livelihoods as the Nile, herds, and fields represented the livelihood to the ancient Egyptians. We, like them, devote significant portions of our lives to our work. In fact, work for many, if not most Americans, is all consuming. For most of us, we *are* our work. We identify and define *who* we are by *what* we do. That is why so many workers "go postal" (i.e., nuts) when they lose their jobs. The loss of the job means a loss of identity. God never intended for us to be defined by what we do. His people are defined by Whose we are!

We are entangled in a demonically-inspired, web or system of "Egyptian" bondage and do not know it. We chase mammon to pay for our overextended, elevated standards of living, and in the process, push out God. Christ, the Author and Creator of Life, desires that He, not our careers and jobs, be the center of our existence. If the removal of them means more time devoted to Him and His purposes, then the Lord will remove them. They are distractions and drains on our time, attention, and affection. Our eternal souls are His primary concern, not the physical well-being, comfort, and sense of purpose and security a career or job can bring.

Toppling America's Military

It is only a matter of time when God will judge America's military since we place so much stock and faith in our nation's military might and power. We are the world's greatest superpower. We have no rivals. We see ourselves as invincible, a force to be reckoned with by all the other nations of the world. God will soon cut us down to size and then cut us off as we continue to trust in our "horses and chariots" rather than in Him.

God drowned Pharaoh's army in the Red Sea. That drowning signified Egypt's loss of military might and force. World renowned for its horse breeding, Egypt bred and built chariots for other nations of the world. The horse and chariot were its chief export. In a single instance, God destroyed the world's standard in military might.

The same fate can overtake the United States when God Almighty is calling the shots. Our drones, missiles, and bombs are no match for Him. There is no human technology that can best Him. With a single word, Christ, the Living Word, can render our bombs ineffective, while allowing our enemies to hit every target in the dark, with their eyes closed ... asleep!

Toppling America's Land and Farmlands

God will destroy those things we see as our source, things we see as sustaining and keeping us. He wants us to see Him as our Sustainer, as our Sustenance, as our All-Sufficient Provider. Crippling droughts, wildfires, mudslides, tornadoes, hurricanes, snowstorms, sinkholes, and floods will continue to ravish our land, especially our farmlands, until we realize God is the One who gives us the ability to create and acquire wealth, not we ourselves, and that we must worship Him, and not what we do for a living.

The epic flooding of the Missouri River in 2011 is a perfect example of God turning America into a wilderness. That catastrophic flood damaged hundreds of thousands of acres of farmland along the river's 2,341-mile route from Montana through North Dakota, South Dakota, Nebraska, Kansas, Iowa, and Missouri, dumping hundreds of thousands of tons of sand on these farms. In the middle of America, a virtual desert wasteland was created! Sand cannot hold nutrients or water the way soil does. So this farmland that was once productive is now unsuitable for growing crops.

In 2012, the extreme heat and lack of rain forced the U.S. Department of Agriculture to declare nearly seventeen hundred counties disasters areas. Approximately 80 percent of the nation's agricultural land is now affected by drought, making the drought of 2012 the most sweeping since late 1956 when only 58 percent of the country was in moderate to extreme drought.

Surely, the time is coming when America will no longer be the Breadbasket of the World. We will be a nation in famine. This is almost unimaginable. But if we do not turn from our greed, covetousness, and pride, God will continue to smite the land with plagues. God will weaken and ultimately destroy our nation's economy and infrastructure, if it means freeing His people from "Egyptian" bondage so they can worship Him as He desires.

Americans are so busy trying to make a living or pursuing the American Dream that we do not have time for God. Our land, like Egypt's, will lie in ruin as a consequence. It was unimaginable to the Egyptians that their land could be reduced to rubble. But it was. It will happen to us as well.

God is Owner. We are Stewards.

We must come to realize that God is the Owner of all things:

- *"The earth is the Lord's and everything in it" (1 Corinthians 10:26, NIV).*
- *"The silver is Mine, and gold is Mine, saith the Lord of hosts" (Haggai 2:8, KJV).*
- *"The earth is the Lord's, and all of its fullness" (Psalm 24:1).*
- *"For every beast of the forest is Mine, and the cattle on a thousand hills ... (Psalm 50:10).*
- *"...for the land is Mine ..." (Leviticus 25:23).*
- *"Indeed, the heaven and the highest heavens belong to the Lord your God, also the earth with all that is in it (Deuteronomy 10:24).*

We are just stewarding what God has entrusted to us. As good stewards, we need to invest His money and resources in those things that please Him. What pleases God?

Loving God and our neighbors as we love ourselves, pleases Him. Sacrificially serving the thirsty, hungry, poor, naked, homeless, widow, orphan, prisoner, and foreigner, captivates our Lord, not growing our 401(k)s. Caring for the poor and defenseless is His "sweet spot."

Tap the Lord's sweet spot and you will see incredible wonders unfold in your life. Your prayers will soar to heaven's heights, and answers will rain down in ways you have not yet seen. Before you can complete your prayer, the Lord will say: "Here I Am!" (Isaiah 58:6). Ignore the poor and defenseless, and you earn God's ire, especially if He has given you resources that you have hoarded on yourself and your family.

A Harbinger of a Massive Economic Meltdown?

Could the recent J.P. Morgan debacle, costing the financial Titan more than $2 billion in losses, be a prophetic harbinger of an even greater economic meltdown than what we experienced in September 2008? Will it weaken the already compromised dollar?

May 14, 2012

Another Colossal Sinking

I wonder if J.P. Morgan's surprise $2 billion loss has any symbolic connection to the surprise sinking of the J.P. Morgan-owned Titanic of 100 years ago. The unexpected, mid-April 2012 loss rocked the U.S. and other national economies. The colossal deficit traced to a UK-based investment unit, headquartered in London. The Titanic was also a British run, Northern Ireland enterprise, although it was owned by the very American, J.P. Morgan.

I strongly suspect the God of the Universe is, yet again, trying to make a point to anyone who is listening. I do not think we have seen the last of this J.P. Morgan fiasco. I suspect we are only again seeing the tip of the iceberg. Expect the unexpected—the sinking of the U.S. economy. Symbolically, speaking it is "twenty minutes to twelve." *(Postscript on August 10, 2012: The JP Morgan loss grew to $5.8 billion.)*

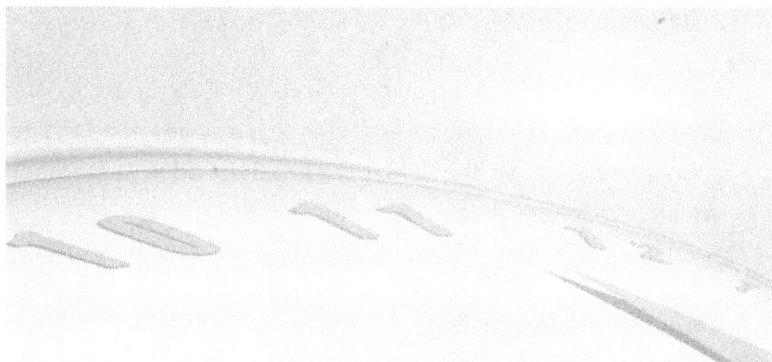

Chapter 19
Argo—A Final Warning!

On March 5, 2013, God woke me up at 4:37 a.m. to talk to me about *Argo*. He put the film in my hand the day before and gave me a day to watch it. The film needed to be returned to the owner that week. I knew the urgent push was from God, not the owner.

I fell asleep that night before we had a chance to talk about the film. But when my eyes popped open in the morning, I heard a Voice in my spirit speak three words: "Ark of Safety." I knew it was God. He was referring to the safety He would provide many in the last hours of the last days, if they heeded His message. They would have to get on board His Ark before His great judgment fell. After hearing the phrase, I remembered the film, *Argo,* a true story.

Argo means "ark" or "ship." The fake film, *Argo*, in the real film *Argo*, represented a type of "ark of safety" for the six American diplomats. They had taken refuge in the Canadian ambassador's home for 86 days during the 1979-81 Iranian hostage crisis. An angry mob had stormed the American Embassy in Iran, demanding the U.S. return their deposed Shah for the crimes he committed against his people. The U.S. refused.

In retaliation, 52 American diplomats were taken hostage. But six others managed to escape to the Canadian Embassy. They took refuge in the Canadian ambassador's home. In grave danger, surrounded by hostile forces, how would the U.S. government get them out safely?

A CIA agent named Tony Mendez devised a plan to produce a fake film on location in Iran. They would convince the Iranian authorities that the six diplomats were part of a Canadian film crew. His bold idea worked. But there was more to the film than the casual observer knew.

On March 21, 2012, a year earlier, God spoke to me about the sinking of the U.S.—a type of Titanic—and the Ark of Safety He would provide His people before its sinking. It would be a time of great danger. His people would be surrounded by hostile forces. At that time, the Lord also spoke to me about Argo—seven months *before* the film *Argo's* release!

March 21, 2012

Hebrew Year 5758/1997: "Season of Noah"

God tells us in Scripture that we can examine the stars of heaven (i.e., constellations) to determine His times and seasons. (This is called Astronomy, not Astrology, which is tied to the occult.)

What would you think if I told you the Hale-Bopp Comet appeared only twice ever, once roughly 4,200 years ago, and again in 1997, in the constellation of Argo, which means Ark/Ship? The first time it appeared was during the great flood in Noah's Day—a time of worldwide judgment—and second time in 1997, the Hebrew Year 5758, which means "Season of Noah."

I would think God is warning His people that the earth is due for another worldwide judgment just like in the days of Noah. I would think the Day of the Lord and Second Coming of Christ are very near since the Lord said His Second Advent would be "like in the days of Noah." I would get right with my Almighty Creator.

In the film, *Argo*, the Iranians were the hostile forces threatening the lives of the six U.S. citizens. Interestingly, the ancient Medo-Persian Empire overthrew Babylon, which seemed impossible at the time since Babylon was impenetrable. The ancient Persians were the forefathers of modern-day Iranians. I suspect Iran and other Middle Eastern regimes will play no small role in sacking the seemingly unconquerable Babylon the Great, the U.S.

In 1997, I began my strange and wondrous journey with the Lord. That same year, President Clinton declassified the Argo operation, making it available to the public. The declassification opened the way for the film, *Argo*, to be made. Neither was a coincidence. The world had entered The Season of Argo—The Season of Noah! Clearly, God, in His mercy, is trying to reach and warn people by any means possible.

Chapter 20
A Cosmic War

*"His tail drew a third of the stars of heaven and
threw them to earth" (Revelation 12:4).*

There is no such thing as happenstance or chance in God's Kingdom. When God spoke the eons (worlds) into existence, everything that would ever be on earth was set to unfold at a set and appointed moment in time. Even the seven strands of hair that fell from my head into the sink this morning as I brushed it were destined for the drain ... at the precise moment they fluttered to the sink. God also knows the exact number of strands left on my head ... and the strands left on the heads of earth's other 7.1 billion residents.

In God's sovereign plan to redeem the planet, He has already considered every good and bad choice that will be made by every human being who will ever walk the face of the earth. His divine, infinite intelligence and capacity defy human understanding. We should stop trying to figure Him out! We cannot! Just believe! He is God! We are not! Do what He says!

He says to us at this hour, "Get ready! I'm coming down to straighten out the mess your choices have made. I AM *not* happy, so it won't be pretty!"

The world is due for another great judgment. It will be tied to Christ's Second Coming, referred to in Scripture as the Day of the Lord. This Day begins with the breaking of the Sixth Seal:

> *I looked when He opened the Sixth Seal, and behold, there was a great earthquake and the sun became black as sackcloth of hair, and the moon became like blood. And the stars of heaven fell to the earth, as a fig tree drops its late figs when it is shaken by a mighty wind. Then the sky receded as a scroll when it is rolled up, and every mountain and island was moved out of its place. And the kings of the earth, the great men, the rich men, the commanders, the mighty men, every slave and every free man, hid themselves in the caves and in the rocks of the mountains, and said to the mountains and rocks, "Fall on us and hide us from the face of Him who sits on the throne and from the wrath of the Lamb! For the great day of His wrath has come, and who is able to stand?" (Revelation 6:12-17).*

This is the dreaded day when God judges *all* rebellion—in heaven and on earth. *"The stars of heaven fell to the earth, as a fig tree drops its late figs when it is shaken by a mighty wind,"* in the above passage refers to Satan and his fallen angels being cast to earth. They are removed from the celestial and atmospheric heavens.

Isaiah 24:21 reveals: "It shall come to pass in that day that the Lord will punish *on high, the host of exalted ones* and *on earth, the kings of the earth*" (emphasis mine). The devil and his cohorts will be ejected from the heavens and thrown to earth; once earth-bound, they will entrap earth's inhabitants in a great delusion.

The cosmic dispute that ensues in heaven may be over the rapture of God's saints. (Remember the story: "Pharaoh" does not want to let God's people leave "Egypt" to go to the "Promised Land.") But Satan and his demonic cohorts will lose the battle:

> *And war broke out in heaven: Michael and his angels fought with the dragon; and the dragon angels fought, but they did not prevail, nor was a place found for them in heaven any longer. So the great dragon was cast out, that serpent of old, call the Devil and Satan, who deceives the whole world; he was cast to earth, and his angels were cast out with him (Revelation 12:7-9).*

Likewise, pointing to the heavenly expulsion are Revelation 12:4 and Revelation 6:13: The dragon's tail drew a third of the stars of heaven and threw them to earth (Revelation 12:4). The stars of heaven fell to the earth, as a fig tree drops its late figs when it is shaken by a mighty wind (Revelation 6:13). In Scripture, angels are often referred to as "heavenly hosts", "starry hosts" or "stars." (See Job 38:7, Judges 5:20, Psalm 33:6, Nehemiah 9:6, Daniel 8:10-11, Daniel 12:3, Revelation 1:20, and Revelation 9:1-2.)

The worldwide judgment will mirror two judgments of the Old Testament. Both foreshadowed Christ's Second Advent. The Lord warned us that His Second Coming would be "as in the days of Noah" (Matthew 24:37, Luke 17:26-27). Yet, He promised never to destroy the earth again by flood. He will not. Fire will remove mass numbers of people from the earth. He keeps His promises.

In Noah's day, "all the foundations of the great deep were broken up" *and* it rained "on the earth for forty days and forty nights" (Genesis 7:11-12). In the Day of the Lord, God's judgment will also come from above and below. The heavens will open to cast Satan and his angels to earth *and* God will shake earth's foundations with a super-quake. The eviction of these demonic forces from the celestial and atmospheric heavens will most likely be accompanied by cosmic disturbances such as falling asteroids, meteors, or other space debris that will shake land *and* sea. (Epic flooding seems inevitable.) This would account for the earth being so violently broken:

> *The earth is violently broken, the earth is split, the earth is shaken exceedingly. The earth shall reel to and fro like a drunkard and shall totter like a hut; its transgression shall be heavy upon it; and it will fall, and not rise again (Isaiah 24:18-20).*

Matthew 24:29, Hebrews 12:26, and Haggai 2:6 also describe this unprecedented shaking of both heaven and earth.

Christ similarly likened His Second Coming to the "days of Sodom and Gomorrah" and their destruction (Luke 17:23-31). The two cities, whose residents were steeped in sexual debauchery, were burned by fire and brimstone (i.e., burning sulfur) sent from heaven! Just before they burned, God blinded the residents. Take heed, this serves as a *spiritual* metaphor for us today!

Many at Christ's Second Coming will be completely blinded to their abominable behavior before a righteous God. They will be lost in their lusts and passions. They want to do what they want to do—when they want to do it, how they want to do it, and with whom they want to do it. Thus, God will do what He must do. Like the unsuspecting, sightless residents of Sodom and Gomorrah, they will suffer a heaven-sent firestorm.

As in the days of Noah and in the days of Sodom and Gomorrah, most people will not heed God's call to repent. They will be eternally doomed when all hell suddenly breaks loose on the earth ... *literally!* The world will be caught up in a cosmic battle between God's angelic hosts and Satan's—a *real* 'Star Wars' battle! (Again, the term "stars" is metaphoric for angels. It should also be noted again that God's mass ejection of these devils most likely will be accompanied by other cosmic disturbances such as falling meteors and asteroids.)

Know that Satan has planned for his eviction. He and his angels will come to earth disguised as "aliens" or "hyper intelligent beings" and they will wrest earth's rein from human rulers. They will ensnare the whole world with their deceptions:

> *Fear and the pit and the snare are upon you, O inhabitant of the earth. And it shall be that he who flees from the noise of fear shall fall into a pit, and he who comes up from the midst of the pit shall be caught in a snare (Isaiah 24:17-18).*

UFOs are not the made-up fantasy of overactive imaginations. Satan and his legions have been actively preparing the minds of the human masses to receive such a deception for at least the past six decades. Satan knew he would be cast from heaven to earth. He prepared for the boot.

Interestingly, the United States—the world's Golden Empire at the age's end—appears to be a special target of God's ambush: "I have laid a snare for you; you have, indeed, been trapped, O Babylon, and you were not aware; you have been found and also caught, because you have contended against the Lord" (Jeremiah 50:23-24). It is this writer's opinion that God will use Babylon (U.S.) to ensnare the entire world. In fact, the divine ambush is already in play.

Satan will incarnate Barack Hussein Obama, who was elected the 44th President of the United States of America by American citizens. The American people gave the "little horn" his crown (Revelation 6:1-2). Obama *is* the future Antichrist. Satan—in Obama's skin—will convince the world with great signs and wonders, that he is God. This grand deception leads to The Great Apostasy or "falling away" of which the Apostle Paul warns believers in 2 Thessalonians 2:1-12.

The body of Christ, the True Church, is not appointed to suffer God's wrath (1 Thessalonians 5:9). Thus, cleansed and purified by trial to match her Head (i.e., Christ), the Lord's bride will have been snatched from earth by this time. In heaven, she will be preparing for the Wedding Feast of the Lamb.

Because Satan knows his time is short, he will wreak havoc on the earth such as the world has never seen. The Restrainer, the Holy Spirit, who indwells Christ's believers, will have been removed from the earth. Unrestrained, the Antichrist and his 10-nation confederacy, will turn the planet into an utter wasteland, nearly destroying it.

By incarnating an assassinated, but seemingly "resurrected" Obama, Satan will sit in the most powerful seat on earth. A supernatural being, the Lord's wily nemesis will employ a host of supernatural signs and wonders to deceive many into compliance. People must take his mark, 666, in the hope of surviving the chaos. But anyone who takes the mark of the beast will lose his or her eternal soul (Revelation 14:9-19).

This man of war will turn the cities of the world into a wilderness. Blood will flow in the streets, famine will grip once prosperous nations, and death will follow. Hades will swallow the spiritually unprepared—those who do not know God and His Son Jesus Christ. Israel will be the Antichrist's special target. In addition, all those who are believers in Christ, before and after the rapture, will be persecuted.

Mass Demonic Possession Paves the Way

The masses will marvel after the Antichrist, believing his deceptions because they will have never before seen anyone or anything like him. Demon possession of human beings that is quite commonplace nowadays, will become even more prevalent during the last years. Only people will now see the actual beings, which from my dreams, appear quite hideous! Masses of people will be driven to engage in insane behavior. A recent dream the Lord gave me confirmed this.

June 9, 2013

A Dream: The Proliferation of Demonic Possession

I just woke up from a dream that confirms everything the Lord has been revealing to me the past two days. I can hardly believe what is happening. We will now see a proliferation of demon possession, leading up to mass-scale control of unsuspecting people.

In the dream, I was seated in a crowded movie theatre. Only the entertainment was not on the big screen. It was live in what appeared to be a circus arena below. (In God's view, much of what we watch on popular media is akin to a circus performance.)

I was member of the audience, sitting in an aisle seat with a male friend seated next to me. We were in the far-right section of the theatre that had three sections—two on either end, one in the middle. We were watching the "circus" below when a fight broke out in the middle section, a few rows above where we were seated.

My friend and several other men jumped from their seats and ran to stop it. The theater management joined the fray. Soon the fighting parties were separated. I turned my attention back to the activity in the arena.

Shortly after that, I saw a young man in a grey wedding tuxedo with tails come angrily down the stairs. Apparently, he was one of the fighters being ejected from the theater. He had a metal sign in his hand. Although there was a great deal of graffiti on the sign, the predominant message on the sign was the word, "Closed," written in cursive writing.

Soon the young bride followed the groom in her long wedding gown. She had flowers in her hair and carried a bouquet in her hand. I watched her as she exited. She mocked the groom as she left. The two had been the source of the disruption.

After a few minutes, shouting came from the very same section where the fight had broken out previously. In fact, a shouting man stood right next to the two chairs emptied by the ejected couple. I saw the man become increasingly more agitated. Nobody moved.

Suddenly, now completely irrational, the man turned to a woman two seats away and grabbed her as if she were his hostage. He put one hand over her mouth and the other around her neck. The woman's eyes bulged in terror.

I screamed to the people standing next to them to stop him, to do something. One woman tried to lift the man's hand from over the woman's mouth, but it was a weak attempt. The rest of the people just stood paralyzed in fear. Defiantly, I rose from my seat and scrambled up the stairs to fight the attacker myself. The dream ended.

The moment my eyes popped open I knew exactly what the dream meant. People familiar with spiritual warfare will also readily recognize what happened in the dream. A demonic spirit of anger and conflict had taken possession of the young groom, provoking anger and the desire to fight his new wife. Once he was removed and she left, the spirit jumped on the next nearest person, causing the same agitated behavior.

In spiritual warfare, a brawling person may be *physically* removed, restrained, or brought under control. But the *spirit* provoking that person to brawl is not contained. Spiritual attacks must be fought with spiritual weapons. Physical force does not solve the problem. The demonic spirit can jump from one person to another. It can cause havoc anywhere it goes. In this case, it was the movie theater.

The spirit can also choose to remain on its original host and travel with him or her, provoking the person to wreak mayhem and destruction wherever he or she goes. The spirit can speak to its host, convincing the person that certain other people must be destroyed or murdered—even loved ones. The spirit will convince their hosts that certain people are not who they appear to be and must be eliminated. While no one was murdered in my dream, the demonic spirit managed to split a newly married couple and caused another woman to be taken hostage.

The spirit is from hell and its intent is to bring hell to earth's inhabitants. A demon will find an unsuspecting host, possess the person, and then proceed to drive him or her mad with irrational fears, anger, thoughts, and voices. People with previous mental issues are most susceptible to possession. However, a person with no history of mental illness or criminal activity can be taken captive by a spirit. A person filled with God's Spirit is not susceptible to demon possession. A demon cannot enter where God's Spirit lives. It can harass and oppress, but not possess.

The Lord and I have had numerous discussions about the explosion of demonic possession in the U.S., acted out in American streets and public venues. Thus, the nation is now experiencing a wave of multiple mass murder attempts in theaters, schools, universities, churches, malls, places of work, and in the open streets.

Not surprisingly, an increasing number of American citizens are afraid to congregate or assemble in public places. They do not know who will emerge next with an assault weapon to slay innocent bystanders. More people want to carry guns to defend themselves. But guns do not get to the root cause. A spirit cannot be stopped by a gun. One may slay the host, temporarily stopping the mayhem being carried out at the moment through the person, but the spirit lives on. It moves to another host. It can only be arrested using the spiritual weapons Christ has given us such as warfare prayers and fasting.

The demon in my dream was determined to bring chaos to people's lives. Hence, the young groom holding up the closed sign. No matter how many disruptive patrons the management removed, the spirit was determined to shut down the place. My scrambling from my seat to intervene at the end of the dream pointed to my understanding of what was needed to arrest the spirit agitating the man.

Mass demonic possession will play a large role in man's falling away from God. Man's worship of God will be cut off, en masse. It will shift to an imposter.

"They Will Mingle with the Seed of Men"

God gave the Babylonian king, Nebuchadnezzar, a dream of a colossal image whose head was made of fine gold; its chest and arms, of silver; its belly and thighs, of bronze; and its legs, of iron. Its feet—10 toes—were made of iron *and* baked clay. Each part of the image represented a Gentile empire that, in its time, ruled the world under Satan's sway. The head of gold represented Babylon. The silver chest and arms signified Medo-Persia. The bronze thighs symbolized Greece. The iron legs characterized Rome.

The feet with its 10 toes of iron and clay represent the 10 horns (or kings) who will arise in the last days out of the old Roman Empire (Daniel 7:24, Revelation 12:3). Of this kingdom, Daniel prophesized:

And as the toes of the feet were partly of iron and partly of clay, so the kingdom shall be partly strong and partly fragile. As you saw iron mixed with ceramic clay, they will mingle with the seed of men; but they will not adhere to one another, just as iron does not mix with clay (Daniel 2:42-43).

Who are *"they"* in *"they will mingle with the seed of men?"* This reference may point to something more ominous and unthinkable than a contentious coalition of 10 Western and Islamic nations unable to coalesce into a unified body. Could it be this revitalized Roman Empire is an ungodly union of human kings (i.e., seed or progeny of men) and non-human rulers (i.e., alien beings—demons in disguise)? Or worse, have fallen angels, once again, procreated with human beings (i.e., mixed with the seed of men) to produce evil hybrids to do Satan's bidding in the last days—as in the Days of Noah? (See Genesis 6:4). The Bible warns us that during this time of unprecedented tumult, earth's citizens will witness sights and wonders never seen (Matthew 24:24).

God will allow the nightmare to last 3½ years, 42 months, or 1,260 days. It will be His judgment on a rebellious people, who refused His only provision of protection, preservation, and security—Jesus Christ (a.k.a. The Ark of Safety, Plan A, and Dr. Ugly's Son). Millions upon millions will die. When the Death Angel passes over, only those souls covered by the Blood of the Lamb will be eternally saved.

What Next?

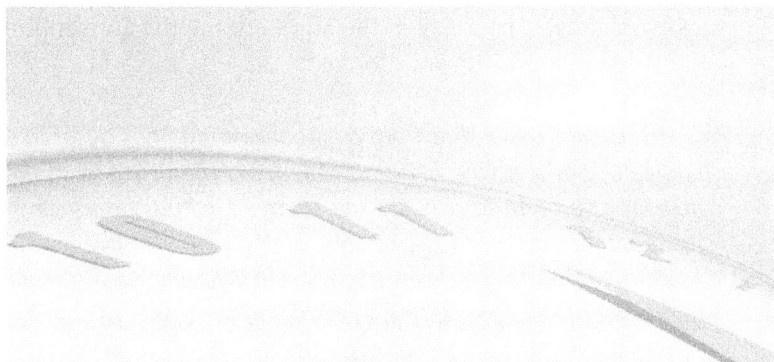

Chapter 21
A Suggested Prayer of Salvation

If after reading the previous chapters of this book and you are ready to accept the free gift of eternal life that Jesus offers you, it is important to acknowledge that your commitment to Christ involves four things:

1. I acknowledge I am a sinner in need of a Savior. This means I repent—turn *away* from sin.
2. I believe in my heart that God raised Jesus from the dead. This means I trust Jesus paid the full penalty for my sins with His shed blood.
3. I confess Jesus as my Lord and my God. In short, this means I surrender control of my life to Jesus.
4. I receive Jesus as my Savior forever. This means I accept what God has done *for* me, and *in* me, and what He promised me in His Word.

If it is your sincere desire to receive Jesus into your heart as your personal Lord and Savior, then talk to God from your heart. Here's a suggested prayer, courtesy of the Southern Baptist Convention to be confessed out loud with your tongue:

> *"Lord Jesus, I know that I am a sinner and I do not deserve eternal life. But I believe You died and rose from the grave to make me a new creation and to prepare me to dwell in Your presence forever. Jesus, come into my life, take control of my life, forgive my sins, and save me. I am now placing my trust in You alone for my salvation and I accept Your free gift of eternal life."*

If you prayed that prayer and truly trusted Jesus as your Lord and Savior from your heart, you made the most important decision a human being can make. You have eternal life through Jesus Christ. Tell someone of your decision to follow Christ.

Begin to talk to your heavenly Father from your heart. You can talk to Him as though you were talking to your best friend. You can talk to Him anywhere and about anything. Pour out your fears, challenges, and concerns to Him. He is listening. Read, study, meditate on His Word daily and you will grow spiritually.

If you reside in a nation where Bibles are scarce or illegal, ask God to supernaturally put His written Word in your hand. Then, prepare for a miracle!

We rejoice in what God has done in your life today!

Chapter 22
As an Individual: Do as Christ Did!

"Here I Am! Send Me!"

In the natural world, rarely can an individual produce change within a "sleeping" or corrupted entity. Typically, the person is restricted from making substantive advances. Thus, everything remains status quo within the company, institution, association, agency, organization, nation, state, city, township, family, etc. No matter how passionate an individual member is, if the corporate body refuses to address systemic flaws, an individual can do little to affect change. The person cannot transform the sleeping or corrupted giant.

Thanks be to God, this is *not* the case for a believer in the world, operating within God's kingdom principles! Christ plus one equals an army! It does not matter how sleepy or corrupt the church or environment is around you.

Nothing is impossible for our Lord. He can work mightily through one, just as He can work through 100, 1,000, or 10,000! How it is possible that just 300 Gideonites could slay 120,000 Midianites? There is only one answer: GOD! God will work with and through whoever is available to do His will. No experience is necessary. In fact, sometimes our human experience and knowledge hinder us from understanding matters of the Spirit. The Holy Spirit does the qualifying. "Not by might, nor by power, but by My Spirit, says the Lord Almighty" (Zechariah 4:6).

Become God's Kind of Hero—His "Rock Star"

God is looking for heroes. Our Lord is looking for heroes in the last hours of the last days to help rescue souls. But know the world's heroes cannot do this. Not surprisingly, the world's heroes are often not God's heroes.

What is the true measure of a man or woman in God's eyes? At the end of the day, at the end of life on this planet, people are measured, not by how much they gained, built, or bought. They are measured by how much they gave, sacrificed, and loved.

As human beings, we admire great accomplishments. Daring feats and exploits get our attention—prize-winning athletes at the height of their game, gifted scientists making brilliant discoveries, skillful adventurers conquering hostile territories, talented actors mesmerizing millions on the big screen, savvy industrialists amassing fortunes.

These are the people whom the world adores and admires, even chases and tries to emulate. Many of the world's most celebrated men and women achieve great and glorious things for no one's good, but their own. By God's standards, many of these are not heroes at all. Some are even scoundrels.

In 1923, six of this nation's richest men controlled more wealth than what was in the U.S. Treasury at that time. But not one had a good ending—one lost his fortune, one ended up in prison, one went insane, another committed suicide and so on. Consider the troubled lives of Christina Onassis, John Paul Getty III, and Howard Hughes. There are countless others. These are not God's role models for us. They are not our heroes.

With whom then is our Creator pleased? Who are the *real* heroes in His eyes? At first glance, many of the Rock of Ages' heroes—His "Rock Stars"—seem quite ordinary. They are some of the most obscure people on the planet, achieving the most ordinary things, day in and day out, in the most mundane routines of life. That is what, in fact, makes them extraordinary.

God has this thing about using the "lowly, foolish, and despised" things of the world to confound the "wise, powerful, and mighty" (1 Corinthians 1:27-28). God's heroes are the men and women who have learned they are on earth to serve, not to be served. They know the best way to find themselves is to lose themselves in the service of others. This is a secret most people have yet to learn, and chances are, never will. But for His called-out ones, it is the secret to successful living in this present darkness, where we find ourselves.

The world is a dismal place, in need of much light. Saints, we are called to be points of light in our little patches of the earth. God has strategically placed each of us. He is calling us to shine brightly in the deep night. Collectively, we can cut large swaths of light in the menacing darkness that blankets the world. We live in a hurting world, but by God's grace, our radiance can dispel the murky gloom.

As God designed it, we reach and touch hurting human beings one person at a time—rocking an AIDS baby, repairing a widow's car, being a big brother or sister to a fatherless child, mowing the lawn of a physically-challenged neighbor, visiting the sick and infirm, delivering groceries or medicine to an elderly friend, teaching a child or adult how to read, washing dishes at the local rescue mission, picking up trash in the neighborhood, providing transportation to a stranger. All these individual, selfless acts of kindness make a world of difference.

I can prove it.

Let us assume for argument's sake that Christ's followers are vastly outnumbered, making up only 25 percent of the world's population of 7.1 billion (See Matthew 13:8). That is 1.8 billion people with the potential to yield a supernatural harvest—"some 30-, 60-, and 100-fold." Say only 10 percent of the 25 percent responded to His call. They WOKE UP! Only 10 percent deliberately and intentionally chose to die to self, realizing Christ meant what He said and said what He meant when He commanded: *"Take up your cross daily and follow Me."* Say, they followed in His footsteps of sacrificial serving! That would yield 178 million Spirit-energized, awakened saints for Christ.

If each of these devotees donated just seven hours a week to being one of God's heroes—that is ONE HOUR A DAY. That would result in 1.24 billion hours a week devoted to serving the masses and rescuing souls. This is equivalent to a supernatural-backed labor force of 31 million full-time (i.e., 40 hours per week) kingdom workers in earth's realm! This is the same as mobilizing the populations of the nation's 15 top cities—New York, Los Angeles, Chicago, Houston, Philadelphia, Phoenix, San Antonio, San Diego, Dallas, San Jose, Jacksonville, Indianapolis, Austin, Charlotte, and Fort Worth!

Imagine for a moment God marshalling for His services these major cities' 31 million citizens! Combine this with the fact that one Spirit-filled believer can put a whole troop on the run (Psalm 18:29). And, remember this indomitable force would be the result of God's heroes investing just ONE HOUR a week in God's causes! Imagine what two, three, four, even five hours a week per zealot would yield! The demonic world system would topple! The planet would be a different place!

But be warned.

It costs to be God's kind of hero. There is no personal glory in it—no fame, no fortune, and no monetary profit. The crowds are not watching and cheering you on. In fact, the enemy will stir and rouse up others to oppose you. There will be conflict, opposition.

Chances are nobody is watching except One. But He is the only one who really matters. You have an audience of One to please—the One who put you on earth in the first place, to bring Himself pleasure and glory. Why not fulfill your reason for being?

Being God's kind of hero requires sacrifice. It requires time away from doing those things you like to do and being with people you like to be with. It requires tabling your needs, wants, and desires—putting aside your agenda to help someone else. And chances are that person cannot give you anything in return.

It requires you to push outside your comfort zone to interact with people who are not like you. But life is not about your ease or comfort anyway. It is about easing the burden of a neighbor or stranger and rescuing eternal souls.

Sometimes you have absolutely nothing on earth to gain from it, but a gratifying feeling in the depths of your soul that you have done as God commanded. You have made a difference. Your audience of One is applauding in heaven. He forgets nothing. You honored Him. In due season, He will honor you in the presence of others and bless your faithfulness.

God teaches what it means to be a true servant in His eyes, using the timeless story of Isaac and Rebekah. The story also offers a glimpse of the incomparable dividends associated with being at the Lord's disposal.

December 20, 2012

Modeling Sacrificial Service

Today, I received a beautiful card from Glory of Zion Ministry. The card's cover featured a traveling caravan of camels, loaded with gifts and treasures. I was instantly captivated. There was only one story in all of Scripture that spoke about a caravan of camels laden with treasure. The story is recorded three times in my journals because it is so precious to me.

I prayed before I turned to Genesis 24 to read the story again. Abraham (a type of God) sent his trusted servant Eliezer (a type of Holy Spirit) to find for Isaac (a type of Christ) a bride from among his people. His people lived far away.

Believers in every generation can be sure to glean valuable truths from this story. Our heavenly Father sent the Holy Spirit to faraway earth to prepare a bride for His Son, Christ, our eternal Bridegroom. And at some point, we (His bride) will be snatched from earth and taken to heaven to be with Him.

In the story, Abraham could not be clearer to Eliezer: the woman must "come up" to Canaan, which was a type of Promised Land or heaven. Isaac must not "go down" to Mesopotamia, which represented earth, and thus a type of Egypt, a place of bondage. They were living shadows, patterning the arrangement of a greater marriage to come.

After making a sacred oath to each other, Eliezer, traveled to Mesopotamia with 10 camels laden with abundant treasure. Eliezer was on a mission, looking for Abraham's choice of a bride for Isaac. He was not seeking someone beautiful or smart. The Cinderella he was searching for had to possess a servant's heart. That was the only shoe that would fit. The treasure was for her and her family. Eliezer devised a plan to test the woman's heart. He decided if he asked for a sip of water from the woman and she gave him a sip of water as well as offered to water his camels, he had found "the one."

Hidden from the casual reader is why this was such a perfect test. Watering 10 camels was a lot of work! After a long trip in the desert, one camel could drink up to 25 gallons of water! Surely, a woman would have to have a generous servant's attitude to make such a sacrificial offer.

Rebekah passed the test! After giving Eliezer water, she offered to water his camels. He had found Isaac's bride! Eliezer immediately pulled out a golden nose ring and two bracelets for her wrists. Later, he showered her with jewelry of silver and gold. He gave precious treasure to other members of her family as well. Virtually everything on those 10 camels was hers! Several days later, Rebekah was taken up to Canaan to be Isaac's bride.

At dusk, the caravan of camels approached Canaan. Isaac was out in the fields meditating. Isaac saw the camels returning with much treasure: "... and he lifted his eyes and looked, and there, the camels were coming ...." But the biggest treasure of all was his bride.

Most people miss the important role the camels played in the Isaac-Rebekah story. The camels point to a hidden spiritual truth under the New Covenant of Christ. Abraham's choice of bride for his long-awaited, "resurrected" son had to have a servant's heart. She reflected the bride God would choose for the "Greater Isaac to come"—Jesus Christ.

Unbeknown to Rebekah, she had to serve the camels to pass the Cinderella test. After she served the camels, the camels served her! The camels brought treasure to her and her family. More importantly, the camels carried Rebekah to Isaac and to a brand new life with her new husband.

Thus, the camels in the story symbolize a sacrificial service opportunity for the believer. If a believer wishes to capture God's heart, the person needs to look for the sacrificial service opportunity

God has put in his or her midst. It will be a heavenly-orchestrated opportunity to show sacrificial love.

Our human tendency is to shun such opportunities. Most of us would not even consider them opportunities. They appear to be burdensome inconveniences that complicate our lives, pull us away from what we like to do, sap our strength and resources, and generally slow us down. Most of us want to do the easy stuff for God, if we do anything at all.

Think about what a camel represents. They chew and spit cud, which is disgusting. They stink. They dwell in the desert. A desert is a hard, rough, and barren place to live. But if God calls us to serve a stubborn, stinking, cud-chewing, spitting camel, then the desert is where we must dwell. We should embrace our "camels"—not shun or flee them. They bring to us treasure. They also have a way of transporting us into the presence of the Son, the King of kings.

God has put camels in your midst. These stinky challenges and nuisances are meant to bring you abundant blessings. Our Creator arranged it that way. In His infinite and incomparable wisdom, He made it more blessed to give than to receive. So when you give, He takes note, especially when you give sacrificially. Consequently, no person can sincerely help another without helping him or herself. You sow into God's fields, you are certain to reap a harvest in due season.

There are many noble, but difficult things that will never get done on earth if you do not do them! Related to this, there are many astoundingly wonderful experiences and blessings you will never experience, if you squirrel away your God-given gifts, talents, and resources for just you and yours. Each of us—no matter who we are, where we are, what we are, how we are—has been called to this time, space, and place, to this generation to make a helpful difference to somebody.

Those who do not step up, who do not give back, may argue, "It's not my camel! Besides, I'm just one person." To the world, you may be just one person, but to one person you may be the whole world, a hero. You may be that *one* person, who can make *all* the difference.

The Power of One

On Thursday, August 26, 1999, a young man with a backpack strapped to his back jumped the security gate at Chicago's O'Hare International Airport. He mumbled something about being late. Airport officials thought he could be *anybody*, including a terrorist.

Rather than chance it, United Airlines shut down all its terminals. This was a hub city for United, so it ushered thousands of flyers out the terminal onto the streets. The next day, an aerial shot in *USA Today* showed nearly 7,000 travelers outside the United Terminal; it happened to be the first terminal at O'Hare. This massive horde of United Airlines' passengers blocked thousands of other travelers trying to get to other airlines.

The airport authorities searched and searched for the young man with the backpack, but they never found him. In the meantime, thousands of travelers missed their flights. And because O'Hare was the third busiest airport in the world at the time, the incident had the ripple effect of disrupting flights throughout the entire country.

Flights had to be rerouted, delayed, and even canceled. Tens of thousands of travelers in cities across the nation were late, stranded, or grossly inconvenienced because of the actions of a single young man. Who can calculate the impact of those travelers arriving late to their destinations or not showing up at all?

Behold, the power of one!

The Power of Personal Influence

Let us look at this principle within a positive context. We all have *tremendous* God-given power of which we are not aware. We can, as singular human beings, influence situations, circumstances, and even the entire world for good (or bad), in ways we cannot imagine.

We each have a sphere of things for which we are directly accountable and responsible. But we also have a sphere of things, for which we are not directly accountable or responsible, but over which we can wield great influence. These are situations we can influence for good or bad. If we are not careful, if we are not cognizant of this power, two things will result:

First, we will *overestimate* our sphere of no impact. These are situations over which we *think* we have no control, no power. We will abdicate matters we ought not to abdicate. We will walk away from circumstances that have been awaiting our arrival. If we are not careful, our attitude will be: "It's not my affair! It's not my business! I can't do anything!"

Second, we will grossly *underestimate* our sphere of influence. That is, we will walk away from settings and situations over which we can wield great *influence* for a positive change or outcome. And when we do this, everybody loses. We lose in ways we cannot even fathom this side of heaven. Most change that occurs in the world does not come from the sphere for which we are directly accountable or responsible. It comes from our sphere of influence! As individuals, we have direct control over very little, but we can influence much for Christ's cause. We must choose to.

God searches the world over for spiritual warriors willing to take Him at His Word, fighters willing to sacrifice, suffer even, for His righteous causes. When He finds a sold-out heart, bent on doing whatever He asks, He will move whoever and whatever in heaven and earth to support that soldier's assignment. He will realign the cosmos—make the sun stand still, if that is what it takes! (I am not kidding! Read Joshua 10:1-15 and check it out for yourself!) For those of you who are still doubtful, let me share with you a personal story.

Resurrecting Denny's Restaurants—A Cinderella Story

On April 1, 1995, almost like an April Fools' joke, I received a call from Jim Adamson, the new Chairman of Advantica, (formerly Flagstar Companies), parent company of Denny's. Denny's was a $2.3 billion company at the time with roughly 1,500 restaurants nationwide. It was America's largest family restaurant chain.

Jim had been there two months when he called me. His request was simple and straightforward, "Ray, would you come help fix Denny's?" Denny's name had become synonymous with racial discrimination. It had become an icon for corporate discrimination, the "poster child" for racial hatred and prejudice. In 1993, it had been hit with two class action lawsuits, totaling $54 million. African American customers claimed widespread systemic discrimination.

When I received Jim's call two years *after* the lawsuits, the company was in tatters, being battered on all sides on the very specific issue of race. Civil rights groups denounced the chain. Denny's was being lampooned in editorial cartoons across the country, berated on radio talk shows, and lambasted in television newscasts. The company had become the butt of jokes for late night talk show hosts.

The marketplace had turned decidedly hostile. Many people refused to patronize the chain. The Company had 70,000 demoralized employees on its hands, who were constantly being tested by an outraged public. Hundreds of workers simply quit on the spot. And as one can imagine, it was difficult to attract new workers to the troubled chain. Hate mail poured in from all parts of the country from every major racial and special interest group. Finally, the company became the "Pariah of Wall Street." Before the lawsuits, the parent company's stock traded between $20 and $23 a share. After the lawsuits, the stocks plummeted to $3 a share. Finally, down to $1.85 a share, the company was kicked off NASDAQ.

When Jim made the request, I had two choices. I could stay in my safe place of smug comfort and simply curse the darkness. Or, I could join forces with those who were attempting to rage against it, to right an ugly wrong. I chose to join the Company's fight. I knew God had raised me up for the challenge. I knew if He put me in a fight, He intended to win it.

Five years later, *Fortune* magazine conducted a survey among 1,200 U.S. companies, looking for the Top 50 "Best Companies in America for African Americans, Hispanic Americans and Asian Americans." The magazine used 16 different measures to determine its ranking—from the demographic composition of the board of directors, senior management team, officer core, workforce, franchise base, supplier base—to philanthropic giving levels and patterns. Denny's ranked Number One. From top to bottom, the Company had become completely inclusive of all peoples. The nation was stunned. Imagine that! From worst to first in just five years!

God did it! He just needed one person to believe in His cause, to believe in His power and might, to believe in His goodness—despite all setbacks—and take Him at His Word. He needed just one person to believe He could do the impossible! God plus one made a majority!

When I said, "Yes!" to God, He realigned the heaven and earth to get the job done, marshalling in whatever and whoever I needed. He created in Himself a formidable team to be reckoned with, and in time, with much struggle, His light dispelled the darkness. We won!

Chapter 23
Getting Started as an Individual

Following are seven precious keys to unlock the doors leading to heaven's most treasured, coveted prize—the King's heart! Win the King's heart and you will *always* have what you need for yourself and to serve others. Your cup will overflow with heavenly provision and blessings.

Key #1: Forget the Past and Press Toward the Prize

The Apostle Paul said, *"The one thing I do: forgetting what is behind and straining toward what is ahead. I press on toward the goal to win the prize for which God has called me heavenward ...."* *(Philippians 3:13-14, NIV)*. Agree with God about your sin, repent of it, accept His forgiveness, and move on. Forget what is behind you. Do not dwell on past failures or past achievements. Learn from your mistakes. Let them fuel your future. Some of your best learning and greatest growth will come from your failures. But do not let your rearview mirror become larger than your windshield.

If you fixate on past failures, despair, and disappointment will overwhelm you. If you dwell too long on past achievements, pride and conceit will overtake you. The past is the past. Leave it there. Forget what is behind.

Strain toward what is ahead of you. Press toward the goal "to win the prize for which God has called us heavenward." You have been placed on this earth for a purpose. No one is here by accident. God is much too purposeful for that. You have been placed in this time and generation for a reason. The goal is to fulfill your reason for being in the time you have been allotted on earth, remembering you are not here for yourself.

God is using this present dark world as your "making place." He is preparing and grooming you for an eternity with Him. Just as He prepared you in your mother's womb with eyes, ears, a mouth, a nose, hands, and feet to negotiate this present world, He is employing the unpleasantness of today's world to prepare you for the next. You are being made to rule with Christ on the other side of this mess.

You can look and see we are living in a usurper's wasteland. Do not be deceived. This is not the endgame. At the appointed time, God will judge the nations of the world and Satan. Your goal is be present and accounted for in heaven when that happens.

In the small window of opportunity Christ has given you as a temporary resident of earth, you must discover that cause outside yourself that is larger than yourself and pour yourself into it for Christ's sake. It usually reveals itself as a burden on your heart or a consuming passion that keeps you awake at night. You dream about how things can be different.

You have God-given interests and talents that your Creator deposited within you. He desires to align your interests, talents, and gifts with your appointed calling. Your talents were never meant to be hoarded for yourself. God meant for them to be given away. He intended you to be a gift to the world as Christ was a gift.

The word strain in the Apostle Paul's counsel to us, offers a clue that whatever God is calling you to will not be easy. Things in life that are noble and worth doing are rarely easy. The word strain suggests that to fulfill your purpose in life, you will struggle, toil, labor, and endure hardship. That is what Christ meant when He said, *"If anyone desires to come after Me, let him deny himself, and take up his cross daily, and follow Me" (Luke 9:23).* He warned *"… narrow is the gate and difficult is the way which leads to life and there are few who find it" (Matthew 7:14).*

There is no one on earth like you, who God is calling to do your assignment. Christ was called to be the Savior of the world. No one could answer that call but Him. No one else can answer your call but you.

You are who you are. You are a peculiar person, set apart by God for His splendid end-time objectives. He arranged it that way. You can stop trying to be like the world. Instead, you must come out of it, spiritually. You must be who God called you to be. You are not like everyone else. God never intended for you to fit into a mold. He never called you to behave like the culture around you and stockpile what He has given you for your own personal gain or pleasure.

Instead, *strain* to discover the Christ in you, and then like Him, give yourself away to a world that desperately needs you. The world is a sinister place and you have been raised up for such a time as this to oppose great looming evil. A bountiful harvest awaits those willing to die to self. The Lord of the Harvest is the matchless, magnificent Prize. What He has prepared for those who love Him, no human mind has ever conceived (1 Corinthians 2:9).

Key#2: Guard Your Mind

The majority of all spiritual warfare takes place between your two ears. That is to say, the spiritual war surrounding you takes place mostly in your head. Satan lives to attack your mind. He speaks deceptions to it. If he can take your mind captive, then he has you. You will be his puppet, doing his bidding and not God's. You become like a circus elephant!

When circus trainers bring in an elephant from the wild jungles of India or Africa, they attach a massive chain to one of the elephant's legs. They attach the other end to a long stake, driven deep in the ground. No matter how hard the elephant tries, and sometimes it tries for days, it cannot get away. Its leg can become bloodied from trying to escape.

After about three days, the chain is replaced with a rope. The trainer ties one rope's end to the elephant's leg and slips the other end over a peg in the ground—a peg! That elephant does not attempt to escape because it *thinks* it cannot. Elephants have been known to perish in circus fires because they believe they are bolted and bound where they stand.

In so many ways you, too, can be like a circus elephant, bound by thoughts and beliefs about yourself, others, and the world that are not true. Most people are often bound by wrong, destructive beliefs and patterns of thinking gleaned from popular culture. Who do you think manipulates and controls popular media? (Get rid of the television!)

Satan makes you believe you are limited, confined, and bound by your circumstances, by what the world *is,* not by what it could be. He focuses you on the obstacles, problems, challenges—the mountains.

But we need to look to the Mountain Mover and His powerful promises. Our Lord is earth's marvelous Way Maker.

Satan is the world's prince and has filled the earth with every kind of deceptive message and false report to keep you bound where you stand. The truth of the matter is you and I have incredible power as individuals to dismantle his iniquitous kingdom and to accomplish extraordinary things for God's in our lifetimes.

The world does not have to be as depraved as it is. Our God is much too big for that. The problem lies with us. The body of Christ has abdicated assignments she should not have. Her members have forgotten they serve a mighty God for whom nothing is impossible. We must take the handcuffs off God! Take Him out of our tiny boxes!

What the mind believes is a very powerful thing. What you *truly* believe determines what you do. Believe God. His Word is true. If you trust it, you will not be disappointed. You will not be put to shame. His teachings are not just words on a page. They are Life! Jesus Christ is God, the Living Word. Choose to believe every single promise in His Holy Writ, despite what your senses or others tell you to the contrary.

Take that so-called expert's opinion to God. What does God say about your circumstance? What is *His* report? Never take another human being's report over God's. God's promises are active and alive and will not return to Him empty. His Word will accomplish everything He sent it out to do. He stands over it to perform it (Isaiah 55:11). If He said it, that settles it. It is finished!

Key #3: Demolish Lies About Race

Satan uses race to divide and weaken us and our efforts for Christ. DNA evidence shows race does not exist. (That probably got your attention.) Geneticists confirm there is more genetic variation *within* racial groups than *outside* racial groups. There is virtually no difference between us underneath our skin. Again, race is a human construct the devil uses quite adroitly to keep people, including the body of Christ, divided. We all hail from one race, the human race. Eve is the mother of us all!

The human body responds the same to outside stimuli regardless of your skin color. If you overfeed, underfeed, burn, cut or puncture it, a human body covered in white skin will respond exactly the same as one covered in black, brown, red, or yellow skin. The result is the same. If overtime you pollute it with cigarette smoke, drown it in alcohol, weigh it down with stress, fail to exercise it, or not give it enough rest, you suffer health failures. Your body malfunctions. It breaks down, gives out, cracks up, and conks out. The human body can falter. It can fail. It can stop working, regardless of your skin's pigmentation.

Because we live in a society, a nation where race has been a very violent and painful part of its history and remains a chief stumbling block for many of its citizens, weird things have resulted. Patterns of disparity have emerged, based on skin color. And because we have not been mindful of these patterns overtime, they have become ingrained in our laws, structures, systems, and ways of seeing and doing things. Some have become so entrenched, so systemic, we are now blind to them in our day to day operations. Satan, the author of confusion and chaos, exploits these disparities at every turn. Like a fiddle, he plays us on all sides! Divide and conquer is his modus operandi.

Today, the vast majority of American institutions and industries—housing, employment, public and private education, banking and lending, judicial and penal, trade and commerce, healthcare, military, media, the arts and entertainment and so on—are upside-down on this issue of race. The Church is not exempt.

Most of God's people are more aligned with the world's view on race than with God's Word. The U.S. Church is woefully out of touch with God's plans and purposes for her as a united diverse body in our segregated world. Rather than rage against the darkness, she has joined it, grossly diminishing her reason for being. Should we continue along this path and fail to make the necessary course corrections, we will become completely useless to God.

There is a race gap in the way America cares for, responds to, and treats her various citizens. It is interwoven into the very fiber of the culture. The disparities in America's laws, systems, structures, and institutions are real and an indictment on the nation, but the U.S. Church does not have to be like the nation. She must come out of the world, be different from the world, or suffer the same consequences as the world!

Key #4: Pray Prayers that Work

In our quest to do as God commanded, consider the biggest factor in this equation—your prayers to the Commander in Chief. He has the bird's-eye view of the battlefield. He sees you in relationship to everyone and everything else on the planet. You do not have to go *down* to "Egypt" get help for anything—ever! God hates that! He wants you to look up to Him for everything you need.

God tells us the prayers of an earnest, righteous person can accomplish much. Some of the most powerful requests you can make are in God's Word. Praying God's Word is the best, most effective way to entreat Him because His Word will not return to Him void (Isaiah 55:11). He stands over His promises to perform them. Say what God says! Agree with Him! If you proclaim a matter as God declared it, that thing will be established for you (Job 22:28).

When you pray, do so in faith. Faith is, not believing God *can* do it. Faith is, believing God *will* do it. If you find a promise in the Word of God, stand on it. Then wait and watch. God will perform it!

Consider this:

IF ...

God controls all things...

God is capable of all things...

You have access to Him through Christ...

You pray with right motives to glorify God...

You pray according to His good and perfect will...

You pray in faith, believing He hears and will answer...

You have clean hands and a pure heart (no unconfessed sin)...

THEN...

Who or what can keep your request from becoming a reality? No one and nothing—only YOU! So pray! Just remember sometimes when God hears your prayers, He often answers them in a God-size way, in a manner that exceeds anything you could ever hope for or imagine. His ways are not your ways. His thoughts are not your thoughts. He connects dots at the cosmic level. You connect them at the ant level. See the difference?

Sometimes it seems as though He does not hear you. Oh, but He hears. He hears everything. He sees everything. He knows everything. And He is working out everything—every last detail for His glory and for the highest good of His Kingdom and you!

Frequently, we do not know what is best for us, so we pray amiss. God understands. His answers are always in keeping with His sacred plans and purposes for us as individuals and for mankind's redemption. In *The Tale of Three Trees* by the prolific Christian author of children's books, Angela Elwell Hunt, I discovered the best example of how God often answers our prayers:

The Tale of Three Trees
By Angela Elwell Hunt

Once there were three trees on a hill in the woods. They were discussing their hopes and dreams when the first tree said, "Someday I hope to be a treasure chest. I could be filled with gold, silver and precious gems. I could be decorated with intricate carving and everyone would see the beauty."

Then the second tree said, "Someday I will be a mighty ship. I will take kings and queens across the waters and sail to the corners of the world. Everyone will feel safe in me because of the strength of my hull."

Finally, the third tree said, "I want to grow to be the tallest and straightest tree in the forest. People will see me on top of the hill and look up to my branches and think of the heavens and God and how close to them I am reaching. I will be the greatest tree of all time and people will always remember me."

After a few years of praying that their dreams would come true, a group of woodsmen came upon the trees. When one came to the first tree he said, "This looks like a strong tree, I think I should be able to sell the wood to a carpenter." And he began cutting it down. The tree was happy, because He knew that the carpenter would make him into a treasure chest.

At the second tree the woodsman said, "This looks like a strong tree. I should be able to sell it to the shipyard." The second tree was happy because he knew he was on his way to becoming a mighty ship.

When the woodsmen came upon the third tree, the tree was frightened because he knew that if they cut him down his dreams would not come true. One of the woodsmen said, "I don't need anything special from my tree, I'll take this one." And he cut it down.

When the first tree arrived at the carpenter's, he was made into a feed box for animals. He was then placed in a barn and filled with hay. This was not at all what he had prayed for. The second tree was cut and made into a small fishing boat. His dreams of being a mighty ship and carrying kings had come to an end. The third tree was cut into large pieces and left alone in the dark.

The years went by, and the trees forgot about their dreams. Then one day, a man and woman came to the barn. She gave birth and they placed the baby in the hay in the feed box that was made from the first tree. The man wished that he could have made a crib for the baby, but this manger would have to do. The tree could feel the importance of this event and knew that it had held the greatest treasure of all time.

Years later, a group of men got in the fishing boat made from the second tree. One of them was tired and went to sleep. While they were out on the water, a great storm arose and the tree did not think it was strong enough to keep the men safe. The men woke the sleeping man, and He stood and said "Peace" and the storm stopped. At this time, the tree knew that it had carried the King of kings in its boat.

Finally, someone came and got the third tree. It was carried through the streets as the people mocked the man who was carrying it. When they came to a stop, the man was nailed to the tree and raised in the air to die at the top of a hill. When Sunday came, the tree came to realize that it was strong enough to stand at the top of the hill and be as close to God as was possible, because Jesus had been crucified on it.

God-size answers to prayer take time. Some prayers God will answer in an instant, in a few hours, in a day, a week, a month, a year and so on. But some prayers take longer to answer because God is moving heaven and earth to grant your request. But He is doing it in such a way that blessings will blow in every direction—not just on you—when His answer rains down. Be patient.

Key #5: *Rule Your Words*

God's Word tells us "life and death are in the tongue" (Proverbs 18:21). The words you speak are powerful! You have more power in you than you know because God's Spirit indwells you. So be mindful of what you say.

You should not engage in conversations that undermine your prayers. Refrain from speaking negative confessions into your life and into the lives of others. You cannot pray that Billy gets his life together, and then say to a neighbor, "That Billy will never amount to anything!" The devil and his army stand ready to enforce your own words against you and others. Satan is the accuser of the brethren and he will accuse you before God, using your own faithless words. Idle talk gives the enemy ammunition to use against you.

People can speak curses into your life, but they will not stick if there is no cause (Proverbs 26:2). They will stick if there is! If you have sin in your life, deal with it before God. Otherwise, you give Satan legal right to oppress, depress, and harass you.

Ask God if there is anything about your life that displeases Him. He will show you. Act on what He shows you. If you walk according to God's Word, you give Satan no grounds to come against you. You gain heaven's help! God has angels who excel in strength and are equipped to do His commandments (His Word) in the earth (Psalm 103:20). They hearken unto the voice of His Word. Think just for a moment. Who gives the Word a voice in the earth? You do! As you open your mouth to speak, declare, decree, and invoke God's Word, the angels pay heed to it and do it. They fight for you!

God says, where two or three are gathered and can touch and agree, in faith, about a promise, He is in their midst. Christ will release His heavenly hosts (angels) to get it done. The battle is not yours. It is God's! Christ is the Commander of the heavenly hosts, and He dispatches them to do His Word and will in the earth, spoken by you, me … US!

There is life is God's Word as you speak it into the atmosphere. Your answers are in His Word! Satan will do everything to keep you from opening your mouth and speaking it. Surely, God hears and answers your silent prayers. But spoken prayers are more potent. The believer cannot command the enemy or take authority over the atmosphere with tight lips, nor can he lavish the Lord with praise and thanksgiving in the hearing of the holy angels, who learn of God's manifold wisdom through us, His church.

Satan's main tactic is to discourage you. But no matter what your situation looks or feels like, no matter how bad the report, pay tribute to God! You can praise your way out of storms. Praise and thanksgiving are forceful weapons in the kingdom of God. They can banish the enemy and arouse the attention of the Lord, God Almighty.

When your heart or body hurts, it is difficult to honor God. But that is exactly the time to do it! Extolling the Lord for who He is, and what He has done and is doing, attracts heaven's attention, because it is so rare. Praise moves God's hand in your circumstances. So commend Him often!

When you pray, use God's Word. His Word contains His assurances to you. Pray His promises back to Him. God always keeps His promises. You have wandered in the desert long enough! You have gone around that same mountain too long. It is time to go into the Land of Promise. Take hold of whatever God assured you as a believer! Read His Word to discover all that He has pledged!

Words, backed by God's power and authority, have tremendous power to accomplish incredible things in the earth. What you speak as a righteous child of God shall come to pass. The Spirit of the Almighty God indwells you, the same One who spoke the world and all the ages into existence. You have a little bit of Him inside of you. Scripture is replete with examples of just how much sway is in our spoken words:

- Isaac had been tricked into bestowing the blessing of the firstborn upon Jacob, and he could not repeal it once he spoke it, although Esau, his favorite son, begged him to with many tears. Jacob, who was renamed Israel, lived out Isaac's spoken blessing (Genesis 27:30-38).
- Israel (formerly Jacob), on his deathbed, blessed each of his 12 sons. What he spoke over each with his tongue, has been (and is being) lived out by their descendants, even today (Genesis 49:1-28).
- Moses, hundreds of years later, spoke a specific blessing over each of Israel's 12 tribes before they entered the Promised Land. His blessings were (and are) being lived out by their descendants (Deuteronomy 33:1-25).
- Joshua cursed whoever dared to rebuild the walls of Jericho (Joshua 7:26). The curse was very specific. Raising the foundation would cost the life of the person's firstborn, raising the gates would cost the life of his youngest. More than 434 years later, in the days of Elijah and King Ahab, Hiel

tried to rebuild Jericho with the help of his sons. In 1 Kings 16:34, Hiel lost his eldest son upon raising the foundation. He lost his youngest son when he set the gates.

- Elijah spoke and shut up the heavens for 3½ years (1 Kings 17:1). He prayed again and the rain returned (18:1, 41). He passed his mantle to Elisha, who received a double portion of his powerful anointing.

- More than any other prophet, Elisha performed many signs and wonders. Whatever he spoke happened in accordance with God's call on His life. Elisha struck the entire Syrian army with blindness as it was coming against Israel (2 Kings 6:18). He spoke a curse on 42 young men who mocked him after Elijah's departure. In the name of the Lord, Elisha called a curse down on them. Out of nowhere, two bears came and mauled the 42 mocking youths (2 Kings 2:23-24).

The one thing these men had in common is that they were righteous vessels of the Lord. And as such, God entrusted them to speak His word. They walked in His power and authority because they could be entrusted to do His will and not their own. The Lord could trust them with His anointing to do good, and not harm.

When Christ walked the earth, He blessed a woman with alabaster box and surely, she was blessed. He cursed a fig tree and it withered at the root. He spoke healing to countless and they were healed. He spoke to nature and stopped storms. He performed miracles, such as feeding more than 5,000 men, women, and children with only two fish and five loaves of bread. He asked God before the people to bless what He had. He *spoke* all these things into being. We are to follow His example.

God is the same now as He was then. He never changes. In every generation, He looks for righteous men and women upon whom He can place His anointing. Through His Son, He calls all of us to be righteous vessels of noble use. We are set apart for His purposes. It should be every believer's aim to be so close to God that He can speak His word through him or her to make what He needs accomplished, come to pass.

Beseech the Lord to cure your talkativeness. This is meaningless, needless thoughts expressed out loud—idle talk. It is a gateway for more dangerous expressions that Satan seizes and uses against you later. It is not necessary for you and me to express our opinions to others on all matters. Often our thoughtless expressions are judgments of others by which we will be judged (Matthew 7:1, Luke 6:37).

There are two main reasons people talk too much. First, we are undisciplined and lazy in our speech. We do not think about what we say. We just say it. We thoughtlessly speak what comes to our minds. We think talking should be like breathing. It should not. God tells us to be quick to listen and slow to speak (James 1:19). God asks us to guard our tongues against pointless speech.

Second, pride causes us to engage in needless talk. We want to share our opinions with others because we think our views are important to know. We like to inform and teach others. But often God is not in the words we speak. They are our own words. He prefers we remain silent and speak first to Him about what we see or what concerns us. Then, He will instruct us on what to say and do, if anything.

When you are talking, you are not listening. You cannot talk and listen at the same time. Listening is far more useful than chattering. The Bible is filled with admonitions to listen more and speak less.

When you stop talking and start listening, you can hear from God. You can discern what His Spirit is saying to you. Likewise, you can hear what others are saying to you. You can capture the spirit of what is being said, not just the words. Most importantly, when you are not talking, you can hear the thoughts and intentions of your own heart, and you can sort them out with the Lord. The devil wants you to talk a lot. Conversing keeps you busy and distracted.

Your speech should have a good purpose. Endeavor to speak faith-filled words, to confess constructive things. Our God is optimistic and positive. He is not in heaven wringing His hands about anything. You should speak words that encourage, extol, and build up. Avoid words that discourage, disparage, and tear down.

When you speak, you unleash words that help or hurt. God warns our mouths are like armaments. Whenever we open them, we have a choice to influence for good or bad. We either speak for Him or for His enemy.

Negative Uses	Positive Uses
Slander, gossip	Extol, protect
Tear down	Build up, compliment
Joke, jest in harmful way	Joke, jest in helpful way
Lie, exaggerate	Tell the truth
Deceive, hide	Speak openly and truthfully
Speak truth harshly	Speak truth with kindness
Flatter for gain	Speak what is true wisely
Murmur and complain to ourselves and others	Say "all is well" and take issues to God
Curse God, others, and ourselves	Bless God, others, and ourselves
Talk ourselves out of doing good things	Talk ourselves into doing good things

Negative Uses	Positive Uses
Talk ourselves into doing bad	Talk ourselves out of doing bad
Depress others and ourselves	Lift the spirit of others and our own
Discourage others and ourselves	Encourage others and ourselves
Stress others and ourselves	Calm others and ourselves
Confuse issues	Clarify issues
Instill fear	Instill faith
Disparage others and ourselves	Speak who God says they and we are
Put people to sleep, bore them	Wake up people (i.e., excite, inspire)
Recollect events carelessly	Recollect events thoughtfully
Ramble, speak without thinking	Measure our words
Bind people	Free people
Wound	Heal (literally!)
Pray aimlessly	Pray strategically
Create or maintain a negative environment	Create or maintain a positive environment
Glorify yourself or the devil	Glorify God
Slander and condemn God (worst use of tongue)	Praise and worship God (highest use of tongue)

If you grasp the concept of how potent your spoken words are, you will transform your spiritual walk. No man can tame his own tongue (James 3:8). But God can take that little muscle and train it like any other muscle in the body. He can cause your tongue to prosper in support of His goals. By His grace, you can speak powerful, meaningful words and avoid those that inflict harm. When you cannot find anything good or helpful to say, speak nothing at all.

Key #6: Practice Daily Being in God's Presence

Learn to dwell in the Shadow of the Most High. Make Him your habitation. If you spend enough hours in the secret place, a new you will emerge. God will show you yourself, your *true* self—as He sees you. You will mourn your sin. As you learn to live in His presence, daily talking to Him and reading His Word, He will nourish your spirit. In the process, He will transform you into His likeness.

Following are 15 exhortations that will revolutionize your relationship with God as you learn to dwell in His presence:

1. Worship and praise God with your mouth. He loves to hear your tributes, and He loves it when the enemy hears you. Your adoration unleashes His power. Thank Him *before* you see a manifestation and express gratitude for what He has already done.
2. God gives grace to the humble but resists the proud (James 4:6). He needs to see you broken before His throne. Confess your sin. Fall on your face and cry out to Him for what you need.
3. Go ahead, dance before Him like David. He enjoys seeing you worship Him with all your being. He made those hands, arms, and legs to worship Him. So dance... a lot. Your joy gives Him pleasure.
4. As we discussed, choose your words carefully. Watch how you speak and what you say. Your tongue has the power to create or destroy. You can use it to speak a blessing in someone's life or a curse. You can speak blessings and curses into your own life as well. Speak His Word and He will make the world around you align with it.
5. Your mouth speaking His Word is your sword. Use it often, not against people, but against His enemies. The enemies of

God are "authorities, principalities, and spiritual wickedness in high places" (Ephesians 6:12). Satan and his minions fear God's Spirit in you.

6. Lift Him up! Talk of Him! If He is lifted up, He will draw all peoples unto Himself (John 12:32). Share your faith. Tell others what He has done for you! Shout it out! Don't hold back! Others need to hear.

7. Practice showing kindness to others in simple, random acts. Don't wait for a birthday, anniversary, or holiday. Write a letter to that prisoner in lockup. Deposit money in the account of that inmate who has no family. Pick up your neighbor's trash. Cut his grass. Take groceries to that missionary couple around the corner. Pay that stranger's electric bill while you're paying yours. Take sandwiches to the homeless downtown. Spend the day at the church's food pantry, distributing food to the needy. Wash dishes after church on Sundays instead of going home to take a nap. Invite that homeless couple to your house for Thanksgiving. You will discover your missing puzzle pieces, the answer to your issues, in these random acts of love. God has made it so.

8. God desires that you become a true intercessor. When you pray, He wants you to pray for others like you pray for yourself. He wants you to pray as if you are chained with them in their circumstances, their "prison pits." He will cause you to identify with their pain and sorrow on a visceral level, and you will wail before Him as you *feel* their hurt and grief. And when you pray for their release, He will turn your captivity as He turned Job's.

9. Some spirits come out only with prayer *and* fasting. If you pray *and* fast, God will work through you to set captives free. There's even more power at work when you pray and fast in agreement with others! If two, three, four, or all decide to

pray and fast, big blessings—corporate blessings—He will pour out.

10. Study His Word. Don't race through it like a passing tourist. He has treasures hidden there just for you. If you tarry, He will show you. He will reveal deep mysteries of which only His intimates know.

11. Judge no one. There is only One Lawgiver and One Judge. Presume nothing. You see only in part what He sees in total. Love and practice mercy, and He will be merciful to you.

12. Rehearse denying yourself. Practice being dead last. Don't rush to be first in line. Don't rush to snatch that parking space. Don't eat that last slice of pie. Give up your window seat so that family can sit together. You know that woman wants that blouse you have in your hand, put it back. Even better, offer to buy it for her.

13. Live by faith and not by sight. It doesn't matter what report your doctor, lawyer, or banker gives you, check with Him. It doesn't even matter what you see with your eyes, hear with your ears, taste with your mouth, smell with your nose, or feel with your hands, if God says it's something else, believe His report.

14. As a radical act of faith, look around you and find seven "empty vessels"—neighbors or strangers in need. Dare to pour out what you have into them. Don't save or hold back what you have for yourself. God promises that your oil will never run dry! You will come to know Him truly as your Jehovah Jireh—the God who Provides.

15. Rest in Him! Be still and know that He is God. He will give you peace during your raging storm. The battle you're in is not yours. He put you in the fight for His glory, and it is a fight you cannot win on your own. The fight is His. In Him, you must rest. At a set time in the future, He will resurrect your life.

You will rise from the ash heap like a Phoenix, transformed—a newer, sleeker version of your former self. Now, He can use you like never before.

Key #7: Love Your Neighbors (and Enemies), Not Things

If we were to take *every* human being who ever lived and lined them up side by side—the high and the low from every nation, tribe, and tongue; and we abolished all levels and classes of society across every present and past civilization and culture; and we took away every crown, title, rank, grade, station, post, degree, and position that man bestows so that no one could hide behind or raise him or herself above another through heritage, tradition, or possessions; and each person was stripped even of his or her clothing so that there would be no sign of emblem, rank, or standing, what would we have? What would we see?

We would see people as God sees them. We would see His created ones in many different colors, sizes, shapes, and ages. We would see a vast array of people all created equally in His image and all in desperate need of a Savior. This is how God views each one of us.

The Lord does not get caught up in our surroundings and accouterments as we do with ourselves and with one another. All society is built on these trappings! They define and drive virtually everything—who has privilege and entitlement and who does not. They shape and greatly influence our actions, reactions, and interactions with one another. They should not. We should love people regardless of who they are and what they have.

God is Sovereign over all human achievements and exploits. If it was not God's will that a person should have or achieve something, he or she would not. Moreover, God does *everything* for His own good purposes and glory. He orchestrates it all—every detail! Everything in creation is His for him to position and use as He sees fit.

Most often things like title, rank, status, position, and possessions ensnare us. They are incredibly deceitful, beyond our wildest imagination! Beguiled, we chase these things, thinking they will bring us love, security, purpose, and happiness. We honor people who have these, even if they are scoundrels. Satan uses these entrapments to his advantage and our demise.

God looks at the heart to see whether it belongs to Him. All human hearts are wicked, as black as night, until they let in the Savior. If you allow Him in, to live in and through you, He will show you how to love as He loves. His brand of love does not impose conditions; it does not look out for self. If you remain closed, you will rule yourself, and you will succumb to the seductions and traps of the world. You will fall prey to the prince of this world, Satan. Destruction will be your end.

Every human being will go the same way. Death (or the rapture) will eventually overtake each one of us. But while our physical bodies will grow old and die, our souls live on. How each person responds to the Savior's overtures of love determines where he or she will spend eternity—in heaven or hell. Heaven is for those who can, by God's grace, transcend the trinkets and trappings of this present world to see people as God sees them. It is a test no one escapes. Not one.

Heaven-bound saints are servants of the Lord Jesus Christ, and they live not for title, rank, or position. If they achieve these, they are viewed and used as resources and tools to help others and to honor and glorify God. They live to please Him. Let us see ourselves and others—our family, friends, associates, acquaintances, neighbors, and strangers—as God sees us and them. They are human souls.

As you grow in the Lord, God will widen your circle of friends, associates, and acquaintances to include all kinds of people. You will hug, pray with, cry for, eat among, fight for, bet on, and trust in people who you would have never associated with in the early days of your Christian walk. *"Perfect Love casts out fear" (1 John 4:18).*

As Perfect Love pushes you outside your comfort zone, you discover people are people. You come to discover we are all messes—works in progress. We are God's glorious workmanship, unfinished. We do not know God's eternal plans for a soul. We do not know who will end up an Eternal Masterpiece and who will end up an Eternal Ruin. We just need to love one another as God commanded and leave the judging to Him.

In early 2003, after being completely disquieted about the United States entering war with Iraq, the Lord gave me one of the most insightful dreams about loving my enemy:

February 7, 2003

On the Iraqi War

I went to bed downhearted after watching the news. I cried the better part of the night about our country edging closer and closer to war with Iraq. All night, I saw visions of innocent people mutilated in the streets on both sides! How many would perish to solve this conflict?

I mulled over and over in my mind if war was ever justified. I abhor violence of any kind. Then I thought of Hitler. Would it have been wrong not to have stopped him? He massacred millions. On and on I pondered these issues until my spirit was totally disquieted.

Finally, I rose around 4 o'clock in the morning to read Psalm 91. This psalm, assuring God's people of safety amid judgment, gave me enough peace to rest a bit. God kept telling me not to worry, but I was not worried about myself or my family, I was concerned about others. Then I fell asleep, and God gave me the strangest dream.

A Dream: A Loving Enemy

The dream opened with me lying on a gurney. I was fully conscious, not hurt or dead. I was naked underneath a blanket that covered me up to my shoulders. Two al-Qaeda soldiers suddenly appeared on either side of me. They were dressed in all black. Black turbans covered their heads as well as their faces, up to their eyes. They wore long black Islamic tunics. Both had automatic rifles strapped around their shoulders. I remained perfectly still, in utter terror.

Suddenly, I realized what they were doing. They were kissing me on the forehead! Each kissed my forehead several times. They alternated. Then one said, "We have to brand her."

"Oh no! That's going to hurt," I shrieked. I knew branding was a way of identifying a person as a possession or property. I was their prisoner.

By this time, I was sitting straight up on the gurney, still properly covered. Their backs were turned to me as they worked with their branding irons. I was beyond upset.

Unexpectedly, they turned around and plastered a rectangular stencil on the left side of my chest. They pressed and pressed the stencil against my skin. Surprisingly, it didn't hurt. They peeled the stencil away and I looked down to read the word, LOVE. The word was stenciled on my skin in big bold, blue letters. Then they resumed kissing me on my forehead. The dream ended.

These men were dressed like the enemy, but they did not act hostile or adversarial toward me. Instead, they surprised me by their love. What was the Lord trying to show me? Perhaps, we need to look past our differences—even radical religious differences—and love people for who they are, not for what they believe. This is the only way they will ever see God. This is the only way to truly win a war.

Our God is militant, out the box, off the hook when it comes to love. Apparently, He does not care who He loves and brings into His circle— drug addicts, prostitutes, wife beaters, transvestites, gay and lesbians, adulterers, murderers, thieves, vagabonds, liars, child molesters, felons, tax collectors, kidnappers, you and me—all kinds of riff raff! Imagine that! Who in heaven's name does He think He is? He is a Radical Lover, reaching out to the world's rabble! We do well to see people as He sees them and follow in our Master's footsteps.

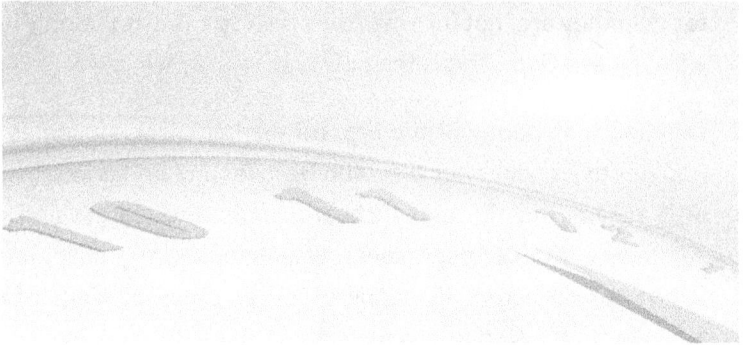

Chapter 24
As a Corporate Body:
Bust Barriers Dividing the Bride!

The Kingdom Case for Unity

First and foremost, Christ's body must unite as one in Him. At this hour, Christ, our Head, is calling us, His bride, to demolish all racial, ethnic, national, cultural, and societal lines of division, including denominational separations. There are *no* denominations in heaven! He is calling for unity where there once was division. Satan uses our differences to weaken us in ways we have not considered or imagined.

We can no longer afford to close ourselves off from one another for whatever reason—fear, hatred, jealousy, ignorance, or pride—believing others' views and efforts are not worthy of consideration or inclusion. Divided, we grieve God's Spirit, and in our flesh and own power, go about our own ways of doing things that are not God's highest and best. We settle for marginal, not even knowing we conceded to something less than what God intended. Not one of us—no branch of Christianity, no single denomination, no race—has cornered the market on spiritual knowledge.

In late 2011, the Lord gave Andre, my husband at the time, one of the most insightful dreams about how He perceives the division between two of the three major branches of Christianity—Orthodox Christianity and Protestantism. (Catholicism represents the third branch.) Andre is considered a "cradle" Orthodox Christian. That means he was raised from birth in Eastern Christian Orthodoxy.

Andre was born in Romania, where 81 percent of the population is Orthodox Christian. In his dream, an old childhood friend, who was raised as a Protestant in Romania, was about to marry a man who was raised Orthodox Christian in Protestant Germany. She was a Lutheran. At the wedding, a fight nearly broke out between the two groups over three trivial matters. The three matters spoke volumes about how God views the split between these two branches of Christianity.

November 30, 2011

Andre's Dream: Battle of the Religious

Andre just came into the living room to relay a dream he had last night. In the dream, an old friend of his, born and raised in Romania, but living and practicing medicine in Germany, was about to get married. Her name is Bridgetta. In the dream, Bridgetta was Lutheran (Protestant) and her husband to be was Orthodox Christian.

The Lutherans in his dream were having a big problem with Bridgetta's Orthodox wedding, in which Father John was the presiding priest. They almost came to blows over three things: the bride's veil, the bride's flower bouquet, and the wedding cake. At points, the Lutherans tried to snatch the bride's veil from her face and grab away her bouquet of flowers.

Andre's dream reveals God's view on this chasm in the Christian faith. We are separated over matters that are not substantive enough in His eyes to warrant the separation. I understand His perspective.

I am presently a member of the Orthodox Church. I was a Protestant for most of my life, and in many ways, I am still one. What I have learned over the past 2½ years as a member of the Orthodox faith is that Protestant and Orthodox Christians embrace the same essential tenets of the Christian faith.

They both agree Jesus Christ was sent from heaven to earth to die for our sins. He was crucified and was resurrected on the third day. He ascended into heaven to sit at the right hand of the Father. He will return in glory to judge the living and the dead. Both groups believe in the Holy Trinity—the Father, Son, and Holy Spirit. Both believe in the infallible Word of God and in Holy Communion.

However, with the help of Satan and our flesh, we have gotten all entangled and divided over unimportant stuff—stuff equivalent in God's eyes to the wedding veil, flowers, and cake. These are things that disappear the day after the wedding. They are no longer useful or needed.

Those caught up in "religion"—men and women who impose flesh-driven rules and regulations versus allowing God's Spirit to indwell and lead them—divide and fight over trivial matters they think are important to God.

Those caught up in a relationship with the Lover of their souls do not have time for religion. They are too preoccupied with God, who sweeps them up in a sweet spiritual adventure. As they journey with Him, they come to learn the frivolity of being religious and let it go.

Sometimes it is not denominationalism that gets in God's way, but patriotism. It is okay to be patriotic, but when patriotism begins to tear at God's family and supersedes what He tells us is right and true, God wants us to choose Him over our nations. Some unwisely put their nations before God. While God will recognize nations in heaven, no nation shall have first place before Him! That is to say, our allegiance is *always* to God first, before it is to any nation. God demonstrated this truth to me in a dream.

December 2, 2008

A Dream: A Sacred Flag

In another dream of the night, I was in a country that was not my own. I felt like a visitor. Suddenly, I saw a huge, white, pristine flag spread out over something. It was the flag of the country. It looked as if it was being sacredly displayed. Although the flag contained a large, vivid-colored emblem, it was mostly white. Then I saw the words embroidered on the emblem. They read: "God First."

I caressed the flag, admiring its texture and the beautiful colors on the emblem. Then I gathered it up and took it into another room and placed it in another spot. I do not know why I did this because during the whole dream, I felt like I was a guest, visiting from another country. What business did I have touching or moving a sacred flag?

Then a priest walked into the room. He was dressed in white. The ceremony was ready to begin. Suddenly, I realized I was in a small waiting room, where a bridal party was preparing for a wedding. The priest signaled for the flag to be attached.

At that point, I discovered the flag was not a flag at all! It was a huge, long, flowing bridal train! It filled every corner of the small waiting room. Two women picked up the top ends of it and attached it to something or Someone. Then they stepped back, away from the train. That is when I saw the bride off to the right of the whole scene!

She was standing quietly, alone against a wall. She looked pensive, nervous. She had a very serious expression on her face. She looked Ethiopian—fine features, big almond-shaped eyes, and medium-length dark hair. Her chocolate complexion stood in stark contrast to her white gown. She looked youthful, like someone's young daughter. The dream ended.

A Heavenly Wedding

God allowed me to glimpse a future scene of His Son's wedding to His daughter (Psalm 45). The wedding appears to take place in heaven. In ancient Hebrew weddings, the bridegroom always wore the train. The longer the train, the more prosperous the groom. (In Isaiah 6:1, we learn the Lord's train is so long that it fills His temple.)

During the wedding ceremony, the bridegroom wraps his bride in his train. In effect, he is telling her that everything she will ever need is in his train. In my dream, the sacred train belonged to the Lord! As His bride, Christ is telling us that any and everything we will ever need is in Him.

The big message of the dream, however, is all nations are united under Christ, our Heavenly Bridegroom, and our allegiance is first to Him before it is to our respective nations. No national agenda—then or now—should ever supersede or preempt God's Word or will. No nation comes before Christ. God First!

There is only One who is all powerful, all knowing, all wise—and we are not Him. We *all* need one another. We cannot disassociate ourselves from one another in the mistaken belief that one group, denomination, or branch of Christianity is better than the others or that we have a lock on all there is to know, and there is no benefit in worshipping or collaborating with others who are not like us. We box ourselves in. We box God in. At this hour, we cannot afford it!

It is God's Spirit who binds us together as one. We are One body, in One Spirit, serving One Head, the Messiah of the planet, Jesus Christ. We can no longer pull in our varied and pet directions. We have one cause, one reason—Christ! God is calling us to unify in our diversity under His banner.

His Spirit does not work where there is distrust, disunity, and dissention. His Spirit is quenched where the brethren are divided. He desires to pour out His Spirit on us as we act as One Man in Him, galvanized around one purpose at this hour—the salvation of souls.

A divided house cannot stand. Abraham Lincoln quoted this truth in his presidential acceptance speech in 1858, but there is One greater than he, who said it first (Matthew 12:25, Luke 11:17). *Anything, anything* divided against itself cannot stand. Christ's bride will remain spotted, blemished if her various members remain alienated.

We are in a war, and in any war, we must have allies. Allies with different points of strength can be joined and harnessed for the good of the overall war objective. Since we have an enemy who is hell bent on conquering us through division, our war cry should be: "United we stand, divided we fall!"

If one part of the body is hurting, the whole body hurts. It is human nature ("flesh") to automatically assume that for someone to win, someone must lose. That is a lie from hell's abyss. It is selfish and a superficial way to solve problems. It is also tremendously limiting and shackles the Lord's hands.

We must eradicate, cast down, throw off our pride and seek win-win solutions for the sake of gaining souls. God will astound us at how often we can arrive at positive solutions that satisfy all parties when we seek to, when we desire that outcome from the outset. We must be mindful of one another. When we are, we are mindful of ourselves because we are all one.

God Loves Diversity

We are all one, but we are all different. If God wanted us all to be the same, He would have made us that way. But as He would have it, no two of us are the same. Every single person is like no other on the face of the earth. Yet we are all members of one race, the human race. God is passionate about diversity. The world around us affirms this truth. Examine creation. It is evident God delights and takes pleasure in variety.

Some plants bloom into flowers, others do not. Blooming plants come in all shapes, sizes, colors, and hues. Some are radiant violet, some brilliant red. Others are bright yellow or orange. Some are a blend of two and three colors.

Different variety of flowers have different characteristics that are uniquely their own. Although the rose is beautiful and stately, God also chose to create lilies, daffodils, daisies, and cacti. Some plants flourish on barren rock, some in the arid desert, and some in the hot, humid bush. Still, others thrive best in warm, temperate climates.

There is immense variety in every form of creation—animals, birds, fish, insects, celestial bodies, stars, snowflakes. The pattern holds true for any species of plant or animal, including the human species.

Although we may have difficulty distinguishing between identical twins, God does not. We each are made in His image, uniquely endowed with physical traits, natural talents, abilities, and gifts—both physical and spiritual. We *each* have our own look, personality, manner, and style. We *each* have our own unique way of perceiving and interacting with the world around us. We *each* have our own contributions to make. Each person is irreplaceable. God delights in what He has created in each person. The fact that God is infinitely creative and enjoys variety is indisputable. Who then, are we to take issue with one another's differences?

The Supremacy of Unity

Consider the Law of Unity. It is this: *"The power of the individual is exponentially multiplied by the unity or harmony of the group."* It is a *spiritual* law at work in the invisible realm. We cannot taste, touch, smell, hear, or feel it because it is not a natural or physical law. Nonetheless, it is as real as the Law of Gravity, and like gravity, we can experience its effects.

Although invisible, it can be harnessed for powerful solutions and results. Said another way, we can get a lot farther faster and be more effective working together toward a common goal rather than pulling our separate ways, in different directions, toward different (or same) goals. *And, and* ... there is a synergistic component or benefit to our working together: 2 + 2 no longer equals 4, but 8 or even 16! There is a multiplication factor in unity, where our results prosper exponentially.

In his fascinating book, *The Secret Kingdom*, Pat Robertson makes the most splendid, compelling case for unity in the body of Christ. Robertson demonstrates through Scripture that there is vast power where there is agreement, harmony, and unity among God's people. When the Israelites agreed, and acted as "one man" miracles abounded: the walls of Jericho fell, 300 of Gideon's warriors routed 120,000 Midianites, King David and his army defeated and uprooted powerful nations, including Philistia, Moab, Zobah, Syria, and Edom.

Remember Queen Esther? The exiled Jews in Persia were saved from mass slaughter when they agreed as one to fast and pray for the queen. At great risk to her own life, Esther beseeched the king to repeal an irrevocable decree against the Jews. Esther advised her uncle Mordecai:

Go, gather together all the Jews who are in Susa, and fast for me. Do not eat or drink for three days, night or day. I and my maids will fast as you do. When this is done, I will go to the king, even though it is against the law. And if I perish, I perish (Esther 4:15-16, NIV).

In ancient Persia, to go before the king without being summoned often resulted in the person being beheaded. God went before Esther. She did not perish. Her enemy Haman did.

The empowering effect of unity was not just an Old Testament phenomenon. Jesus Himself promised, *"If two of you on earth agree about anything you ask for, it will be done for you by My Father in heaven. For where two or three come together in My name, there am I with them" (Matthew 18:19-20, NIV).*

While God certainly hears the prayers of individual believers, there is something especially potent about the prayers of two or more believers in agreement. Imagine how heaven would dance if we transcended our racial, ethnic, and denominational boundaries to embrace one another and agree in prayer about evangelizing the world and other righteous causes. Hell would shake.

God's Spirit flourishes mightily where there is unity. The hidden multiplication factor at work defies human explanation, except to say that it is the supernatural power of God. His power explodes!

The first century church, in its infancy, serves as a model of spiritual unity. Initially, a very special unity and oneness characterized Christ's body:

They devoted themselves to the apostles' teaching and to the fellowship, to the breaking of bread and to prayer. Everyone was filled with awe, and many wonders and miraculous signs were done by the apostles. All the believers were together and had everything in common ... and the Lord added to their numbers daily those who were being saved (Acts 2:42-47, NIV).

God gives us His own model. The Holy Trinity presents an ideal model of unity in operation. The glorious Godhead, comprised of Three Persons—Father, Son, and Holy Spirit—operate in flawless harmony as a single unit. They provide an excellent example of how distinct Persons with fundamentally different functions can work together to accomplish extraordinary acts.

There is no competition or rivalry between them. Each Person has an important role within the Godhead. Each operates in perfect accord with the other Two. And so, should it be with us.

It is God's desire that within the body of Christ, there be unity in our diversity. Careful study of Paul's teaching on the gifts of the Spirit clearly shows it is God's desire that we galvanize our different gifts around the common goal of building up the body of Christ:

There are different kinds of gifts, but the same Spirit. There are different kinds of service, but the same Lord. There are different kinds of working, but the same God works all of them in all men. Now to each one the manifestation of the Spirit is given for the common good" (1 Corinthians 12:4-7, NIV).

Every part of the Body has a valuable role to play for Christ's cause:

Now the body is not made up of one part but of many. If the whole body were an eye, where would the sense of hearing be? If the whole body were an ear, where would the sense of smell be? But in fact, God has arranged the parts in the body, every one of them, just as He wanted them to be. If they were all one part, where would the body be? As it is, there are many parts, but one body (1 Corinthians 12:14-20, NIV).

Unity does not mean uniformity. We can all labor differently to save souls, but as we do, we should not devalue or dismiss the parts or functions of the Body that are different from our own. *"The eye can't say to the hand, 'I don't need you!' And the head cannot say to the feet, 'I don't need you!' On the contrary, those parts of the body that seem weaker are indispensable"* (1 Corinthians 12:21-22, NIV).

All the Body's diverse parts must work in loving unity if the Church is to achieve her mission. Francis Schaeffer's *Mark of a Christian* makes the brilliant argument that our coming together in Christ as one is the single, biggest piece of evidence to a fallen, corrupt world that Christ's claim is true. That He is, indeed, God's Son sent to save the world! Regardless of our differences our love for one another marks us as Christians.

Just before His crucifixion, the Lord gave this command to His disciples: *"A new command I give you: love one another. As I have loved, so you must love one another. By this all men will know that you are My disciples, if you love one another"* (John 13:34-35, NIV).

Then later that night He prayed to the Father:

> *... My prayer is not for them alone. I pray also for those who will believe in Me through their message, that all of them may be one, Father, just as You are in Me and I am in You. May they also be in us SO THAT THE WORLD MAY BELIEVE THAT YOU SENT ME (John 17:20-21, NIV, emphasis mine).*

He continued: *"I have given them the glory You gave Me, that they may be one as we are One—I in them and You in Me. May they be brought to COMPLETE UNITY TO LET THE WORLD KNOW THAT YOU SENT ME and have loved them even as You have loved Me"* (John 17:22-23, NIV, emphasis mine). Therefore, our love for one another in *complete* unity signals to a dying world that Christ was sent by His Father to save it.

Unity—A Universal Law

Unity can also be harnessed to inflict enormous harm. It can be exploited to do great evil. Take the Tower of Babel. The charismatic leader Nimrod, in defiance to God's expressed command to multiply and fill the earth, chose to rebel against God. He sought to build a tower as a monument to the people's pride and reputation, a shrine that would reach to the highest heavens.

God confounded the language of the people to stop the tower's construction and to scatter them across the face of the earth. But let us not overlook the Lord's remarkable observation. He marveled: *"Indeed the people are one and they have one language, and this is what they begin to do; now nothing that they propose to do will be withheld from them (Genesis 11:6).* The Antichrist will turn the world into a barren desert as he unites the nations of globe against Christ at the age's end.

Disunity's Downside

Just as there is immense upside in unity, there is a significant downside in disunity. A divisional factor is at work in disunity; it weakens or dilutes results. Where there is disunity and division, it takes twice as long to go half the distance. Yet, in many areas of our public, private, professional, and ministerial lives, we travel separate roads, splintering our talents, gifts, resources, and ideas.

Take the 11 o'clock hour on Sunday morning. Blacks worship here. Whites worship there. Never mind we have the same goals, same values, same standards, same enemy, same Bible, same God and going to the same heaven. But as what—a divided people, a divided body? Do you think God will have black and white neighborhoods in heaven? Banish the thought! What are we doing? Sometimes we need to helicopter upwards to take a good look at ourselves, to see what God sees.

Disunity and dissension between us result in weaknesses. They lead to deficiencies, flaws, short sightedness, and our ultimate collapse. God's Spirit does not operate where there is division. We need, instead, to build bridges of cross-racial, cross-cultural, cross-denominational understanding.

Some may argue, "Well, we've gotten along okay so far." Let me submit to you their vision is too small. God does not want us to just "get along okay." He wants us to seize back, recover what is rightfully ours—the earth and the dominion of it! Christ died for it! It is His! It is *all* His! And as His co-heirs, it is rightfully ours.

We have the authority and power in God to win back what has been stolen. The enemy should not have us on the run! We have the muscle as one in Christ to put him on the run! We do not want the present world as it is with all its trappings and entrapments. We want the souls of men and women out of the world before God judges it. After His judgment, we shall inherit the earth (Psalm 37), and under Christ's headship as Messiah, we will rebuild and restore it to God's original plan.

Already, we have wasted too much. Because of national, ethnic, and racial prejudice, and denominational preferences that promote division, the body of Christ has forfeited a great deal of her true potential—what she could have become, achieved, and contributed to the world. The loss is incalculable—the squander of human energy, talent, and brainpower; the diversion of precious financial and human resources; the forfeiture of multicultural, multiracial, and multidenominational synergies that could have fueled untold kingdom advances and breakthroughs. Our lack of racial, ethnic, and denominational unity has cost us in ways we will never know this side of eternity.

Unity in Diversity—An Untapped Source of Power and Strength

Our diversity, brethren, is an untapped source of strength, power, creativity, and richness for God's kingdom. First, consider the strength unity has in the secular realm alone, where there is no supernatural power, just natural, human energy. The secular, natural world can and does benefit from the unity principle.

Research shows that over the last quarter century more technological advances and leading-edge products and services have come from multicultural, multifunctional partnerships. Increased creativity and innovation are more likely to come from these types of collaborations than from one homogenous group working on the same issue or problem.

Evidence continues to mount that well-managed diverse groups outperform homogeneous groups of the same size. Social psychologist Robert Ziller's review of research studies on small group performance concludes that "well-managed diverse groups quantitatively and qualitatively outperform homogeneous groups, particularly on complex tasks requiring creativity, innovation and problem-solving."[5]

A 1991 study by the Graduate School of Management at UCLA compared the effectiveness of diverse and homogeneous teams. Researchers recorded and charted team effectiveness of both team

---

[5] Robert C. Ziller, "Homogeneity and Heterogeneity of Group Membership," *Experimental Social Psychology*. Holt, Rinehart and Winston, 1972.

types. The result was a distribution of team effectiveness that formed a bell curve (i.e., normal distribution).

The study found that diverse teams, headed by leaders who could galvanize group members around a common goal, were the most effective in solving problems. These leaders recognized and utilized the different team members' strengths. Homogeneous teams—teams where the members were most alike—exhibited average effectiveness in finding solutions to the same challenges. None of the homogeneous teams could match the synergy of the orchestrated diverse teams.

Intriguingly, the teams that were least effective were also the most diverse. A key distinction between the diverse teams that were most effective and those that were least effective traced to the way the team leaders handled differences within their groups. Among the least effective teams, differences were ignored, put down, or devalued. Division, dissension, and disorganization characterized these groups. The goal suffered from their lack of unity. In striking contrast, among the most effective teams, differences were appreciated and harnessed for the common good. These teams outperformed the other team types.

Today, American corporations invest millions of dollars to educate and train their workforce to value and leverage the diversity that surrounds their industries and businesses. They know that increased creativity and innovation are more likely to come from a heterogeneous workforce than from one that is homogeneous. Companies also know they will miss market opportunities if the existing workforce does not learn to manage their differences to support the bottom line.

This is the business case for embracing differences in the natural, secular world to produce WIDGETS (i.e., unimportant stuff)! Imagine for a moment what would happen if we in the body of Christ connected our points of difference and exploited them for the Creator of the Universe, for the salvation of human souls in this last hour! Now we would have tapped into an unimaginable source of power that the world has never seen before. We would be untouchable, unstoppable!

A Powerhouse: A Diverse, United Body Under Christ

We must unify our diversity under Christ! We must unite across our lines of difference to achieve what our Commander in Chief commanded: *"Go ... make disciples of all the nations, baptizing them in the name of the Father and of the Son and of the Holy Spirit, teaching them to observe all things that I have commanded you ...."* *(Matthew 28:18-20).* There is enormous clout in *not* splintering our efforts, financial, and human resources as we answer God's call at this pivotal hour.

The call to us today is to unite across denominations; across racial, ethnic, and cultural divides; across areas of specialization and expertise; across everything that divides us to bring a *real* voice, God's Voice, to the social injustices, disparities, and demonic schemes that ravish the poor, defenseless, and innocent around us. We have been called to actively, vigorously, and dynamically demonstrate Christ's love to a dying world.

Our collaborative partnerships will uncover areas where win-win scenarios are possible to rescue souls from the enemy's clutches. The challenges and dilemmas one group faces are the same ones all groups face. Again, we can be dissimilar, but work together in our own ways to achieve the common goal. It is advantageous that we are distinctive since the souls we seek are as varied as we are different. God will ensure creativity and innovation will spring from our integrated differentiations!

Collectively, with our Lord at the helm, we can map out radical paths to change, unearth influential tools to upsurge our outreach to those living in the margins without Christ. Together, we can birth enemy-confounding strategies to help the blind triumph over Satan's ruses. Life's Author stands ready to instruct His agenda-free body on how to solve some of life's most perplexing problems.

United in Him as one we can eradicate, yes demolish, entrenched institutional systems and structures that daily snuff out people's lives. Jointly, we can establish national and international forums to share best practices and create centers of excellence to serve as models— no testimonies—of what a great and glorious God does when we relinquish our thrones to Him.

It Starts with Humility

Saints, we are our biggest problem. We are our own worst enemy. The route to breaking the barriers that divide us as a body must begin with our humbling ourselves at the foot of God's throne, and then humbling ourselves before one another. Prostrate on our faces, we must repent and ask the Lord's forgiveness for pride that has caused us to split His body. We must confess that our racial, ethnic, national, or cultural arrogance and religious pride has inflicted harm on the body and hurt Christ's cause. We must admit that we do not know what we do not know. We must become teachable if we are to learn anything at all. No one group or denomination alone will solve the spiritual crisis before us. Christ is about to judge the nations and we are fighting over the wedding cake!

God does not suffer Lone Rangers. He deliberately and intentionally made us a living body of interdependent parts. We *all* have valuable things to learn as well as contribute to the good of the whole body. We each have a part to play in unlocking the answers to this hour's painful perplexities. We share the same goals, values, and aspirations.

We share the same issues, problems, and difficulties. Likewise, we share the same God and battle a common enemy.

None of us has cornered the market on receiving divine wisdom and ideas from above. God gives grace to the humble, but He resists the proud (James 4:6). We do not know what we do not know. But together, we can find out as one body joined to the Head, who is all wise and poised to pour out His Spirit on a united Church.

We must come outside of our traditions, cultural constructs, norms, and comfort zones, to explore—better invade—one another's world. The invader or explorer must be welcomed and embraced. No doubt, we will discover we have much in common, even with people we initially perceived to be very different from ourselves.

At this point, fully in God's will, we can beseech Him to do the impossible on our behalf. We can rightfully ask and expect Him to supernaturally sanctify and consecrate our collaborations, partnerships, and alliances for His glory. We will stand astounded as a new world of opportunity for evangelism unfolds before us. God will pour forth a revival the world has never seen, preparing the way for the Second Exodus—the Great Escape out of a terrible time of trouble.

Church, it will happen in this order: Repentance ... Reconciliation ... Revival ... Rapture. Beloved, do you know the best part about our all coming together as one in Christ? We *all* win!

SELECTED BIBLIOGRAPHY

Hunt, Angela Elwell. *A Folktale: The Tale of Three Trees*. Oxford: Lion Children's Books, Lion Publishing, 2001.

Lloyd, James. "The Lion, the Bear, and The Leopard - Part 1." *Christian Media Research*. Christian Media Network. January 27, 2003. Web. May 5, 2012.

Robertson, Pat. *The Secret Kingdom*. Dallas, TX. Word Publishing, 1992.

Vallowe, Ed F. *Biblical Mathematics—Keys to Scriptural Numerics*. The Olive Press, Columbia, 1998.

Ziller, Robert C. "Homogeneity and Heterogeneity of Group Membership," *Experimental Social Psychology*. New York: Holt, Rinehart and Winston, 1972.

www.ingramcontent.com/pod-product-compliance
Lightning Source LLC
Chambersburg PA
CBHW060238050426
42448CB00009B/1502